DJ CHRONICLES

DJ CHRONICLES

Love, Life and Beyond the Booth

JD DOMINO

Hard Knocks Publishing

Dedication Page

This is dedicated to my mother, the one that made me grounded and to stay goal oriented. She instilled my moral values and qualities to be a gentleman. We shared some of my stories along my way, growing up in life. Thank god she isn't here to hear these stories. Just because she is no longer with me, I still hear her voice, "Stop this crap, you have two master's in education." Mom, I have a YouTube channel and a website also; however, I am still looking.

FORWARD

by Dave Bartley Bussard

This is a story about finding yourself, learning that what you never thought you could do or even thinking of doing, you suddenly realize you can do it. In DJ Domino's case, he discovered he did it. In his early 20's radio broadcasting and Bar DJ opened his eyes and mind especially being a bar DJ. He found life inside and outside the DJ booth, and sometimes the two worlds could be very different. He found his voice; he learned how to command their attention, which wasn't always easy. Try keeping a bunch of rowdy drunk's calm and happy isn't easy, but Domino figured out just the right way to do it.

This story takes you through it all when you are in your early 20's and thrust into the bar and night club scene. Your eyes are opened really wide, women, sex, lust, alcohol, drugs, brawls, music, money, interesting characters, and lasting friendships. I ought to know because I was there through a part of it with him and let me tell you I was probably more naïve than he. I was this 22-year old who thought he was Micky Dolenz of The Monkees.

I had the pork chop sideburns the hair, and I looked at Domino after watching him do his thing one night, and I said, "Man, I don't know if I can do what you do on the mic." He was already seasoned, and if he wasn't, he sure seemed like it to me. So enjoy JD Domino's journey inside and outside the DJ booth. It's a fun ride you won't want to put the book down.

The Beginning

Did you ever think to yourself, "Why am I doing this, and how did I get here?" All I was doing was evolving to extend my mother's ideal world of education equals a career. I just skated through in high school without much effort, and I did what I needed to do. I was becoming a zombie walking the path my mother has set forth. She asked what college and career path I was looking for, and I thought COLLEGE, WTF. So I played the game, said I want to be a cameraman, was at an event one day, saw a shooter, and thought that job seemed relaxed and comfortable, but I didn't know what it took to become one.

The day finally came, and my high school educational experimental journey has ended. The only college that would take me was the local community college, and I needed to jump through some hoops to be accepted. I got lucky to be enrolled with the County College for communications. The production classes excited me, but the studies sucked. I gravitated to the radio side. I felt this was easy; all I need is two turntables and a microphone to make some money. There go my studies, and all my time was spent at the college radio station.

Through mutual friends, I met a dude [Turn Table Tom] from Trenton State Radio who had a show on Saturday nights. I couldn't get into the alternative music scene and the musicians that created it, but this is where I cut my teeth in "radio." Every Saturday, I would do the news and start getting the production bug by recording show promos.

We had a couple of young ladies that would call and eventually hook up after the show, but my luck, I was 19, and they were underage but fully developed (lucky I was slow on female hints, so I was a good boy), but damn I still remember her digits.

Anyway, working at the TSR, I learned the radio inside hanging, interviewing, and what it takes to develop a show for the masses. Tom would let me pick a song a week (of course, it was something with a beat); this would land me my significant 30-minute dance segment on his show. We would have mixed reviews, but every week the listeners wanted to know if I was on.

I was learning my ear for the masses. I remember one week Tom changed the speed on a turntable (if which was my lead for the show), all of a sudden, I yelled, "WHAT THE FUCK," Tom started to laugh and said, "let it go," so we decided to let it go; whatever the record's speed was, we would use the opposite (45 rpm to 33rpm). That show was the fastest because of the speed change, and we got oodles of phone calls in the positive and wanted to hear this again. College radio is what one can get away with, but one can hone their skills for the next level.

Between working at both college radio stations and not showing up to class, one could come up with, "Maybe college isn't for me." Mom suggested, "Why don't you try broadcasting school." I met the living ledge of local radio, Bill/Singer. Bill was Trenton's voice during the glory days of AM radio; he was a DJ, newscaster, and the voice of speedway on the weekends. Bill had a booming voice that any broadcaster would be envious of. I learned my love for production and plan for a radio show, which helped me out when I started to produce shows. I also learned what it takes to become a good broadcaster from some of the legends of their time. Bill would shop around with some of his contacts in Philly and local radio to see what was open in the market.

I got a job starting as a remote crew engineer, then rolled into a production assistant and then a morning show producer.

I graduated and worked at a radio station in production and had my own DJ Company, and even was invited to teach at the school. So, I never really left the school because I was there about three nights a week teaching and helping Bill out. I didn't realize this would become the foundation of my rock jock days and my pool of DJs I would use during these days. Life is good; I am working part-time in radio and hanging at the school for a carefree 20-year-old; things are about to accelerate in a direction I didn't think I'm ready for. Let's buckle up. This is where I got my education and grew up fast.

"He Said What"

When my father gave me the lecture on some bars, he didn't think it was safe to play at. Since he delivered beer and bartended, he thought he knew the safe spots. A month later, he asked if I wanted to DJ in a bar, and I was interested; he told me the bar's name. I responded, "You told me, do not work or go to this place." He claimed it since then, and it was safe.

I figured what the hell. The best news ever was a classic rock and heavy metal bar. I knew the owner; he was a family friend. The main problem was I was a disco boy and wasn't in the rock scene, especially I wasn't a so-called fan of Led Zeppelin, Pink Floyd, The Doors, Grateful Dead, or The Beatles, to name a few. So let the games begin.

WELCOME

TO

MY WORLD

The Audition

This was my first experience in this kind of environment. I was very inexperienced for my age at 20 and very wet behind the ears in this situation.

I remember only bringing enough records for a couple of hours, which was supposed to be only a 1 ½ hour audition.

I had to borrow records and buy some for this blessed occasion. I had nothing except for dance and top 40; some crossed over but were used as filler, not the main course.

I had a good vibe from the crowd; I went back and forth from classic rock to metal and then some party tones; this joint was rocking.

I didn't realize it that night, but I created my music circle (as they do on the radio). The crowd was singing and bopping in their chairs, and it was crazy. I never experience something like this before.

I was playing songs out of my ass, and it was working. The boss came up to me and said, "Hey Kid, Break it Down; I saw enough." I felt like, what the fuck? I BLEW IT, but I was wrong. All of a sudden, the bar started to chant, "WE WANT MORE." I looked outside the DJ booth, and a customer was stacking up tables and chairs, barricading me in the booth. The old man said, "Give them what they want," and my nerves settled down.

The Party Is Mine

I had a couple of weeks to get more records and ask people what the hell I do with this crowd. I got in response was, "GOOD LUCK, DON'T GET KILLED" I felt like that kid from the "Christmas Story," everybody saying you'll shoot your eye out. I've been going to the bar while the old jock was playing until he left for the shore to understand better what music he plays. This was awkward; I'm sitting here at the bar, and peps are saying, "Why don't you spin and show this guy how to play."

I was approached by one of the regulars, and he asked me, "Do you know why the glass doesn't go to the ground because too many people would be thrown out the glass windows. That's why the bottom half of the building is brick."

Wow, that made me feel at ease. I met my mole, and I knew he would become my insider and helped me get the right music for the whole bar. They called him "Bones," and soon, I would figure where the name came from.

I Went Back to School

I had a couple of days before I took over the bar, so I went to see the golden voice tonight. I stopped by Singer's, where I went to broadcaster school; he told me to come by and wanted me to meet the new students; they were a husband and wife team, Johnny "Hot Traxx" and Brandy Max. Johnny was a character like me, never could shut up, but I like these people and figured this wouldn't be the last time I see them.

Time to Man Up....Welcome to The Rock

It's my first official night at the ROCK, and I was shitting my pants. I entered the bar, and some people remembered me, and it made me somewhat comfortable. I figured let me walk around and get a vibe of what kind of music they like. That became a way to start my playlist. I got into the booth pulling records, and then I saw her; I thought of the Commodores right away (she's a brick house), if you know what I mean. Mr. Game keep looking but was dodging my face so she couldn't see me staring at her, but the rest of the night, I felt her watching me as I was of her.

I gave a solid 4 hours, and Bones kept coming up and saying it sounds good not to hear the same shit every night; now, you must keep up the mix and variety of the artist. Bones was strange in a good way. He liked metal but also enjoyed the classic, and as he said, "You can't forget about the shit that makes a chick shake her ass."

I Grew Some Balls To Night

Tonight, I did my usual walk around the bar, and this time I stopped by and introduced myself to this eye full of candy. I was so smooth that I asked what her favorite music was and told her that if I don't have it tonight, I'll bring it with me tomorrow. She asked, "So do you have Brian Adams, the Pretenders, the Babies, Fleetwood Mac or John Wait?" You know they were on top of my record shopping list the next day.

Here Comes The Welcoming Committee

Here comes Bones with a couple of guys (the mental heads) trying to influence their music, but instead, they are educating in metal because I wasn't strong in that genre.

Next came, George is now different because he was the only black man in the bar. I said, "Excuse me, sir; we don't play that type of music." He responded with, "What do you don't play Led Zeppelin or Marshal Tucker." We laughed, and he said I just wanted to say keep up keeping up.

My One Week Anniversary

Around 11:30, I heard a noise outside my booth; Joe was stacking tables and chairs at the door. The bar said, you're ours now. You can't leave "Happy One Week.

Did I say something?

Tonight, the old man comes up to me after the bar closed and said, "Kid, you have to start talking more on the mic."

I thought I was talking enough to promote the bar's upcoming events. I was shy or just scared to say anything to piss people off on the mic and didn't know what to say. He said I need you to talk to the bar like the other jerk off did.

Promos

I was reading the bar's promotions n said, remember to take care of your bartenders. According to the old man, I would also announce requests, which was a start but not what he wanted. He said you have to spice it up like that dirtbag that was in here before you—these assholes like that shit.

I Think I'm Getting Closer

Tonight, I targeted the bartenders n made them the center of abuse, and it worked, the crowd got into it, and the bartender's tips were better than before.

My first target was Mr. Personality; this guy thought he was little Romeo; he would have the ladies waiting for him to finish.

I made my usual plead to take care of the bartenders for making you so drunk you forget what you brought home with you, especially taking care of Mr. Personality; he has so many devices he needs to support. He will appreciate it; Hum Hums can only go so far.

He took one for the Team

I had a party rock groove going n I played "Tequila." Suddenly, I saw Jr. (the boss's son) jump on the bar and do the Peewee Herman, the bar went crazy, and I started to make him a target on my ammo list.

I saw her again; I decided to find courage since my confidence is getting stronger. I found out she was single and had a kid. WTF, I'm too young for that, but good dam, her body was built for speed.

Hey Jukebox

Tonight I tried something different in turning off the jukebox; usually, I tell the doorman, and he turns it off, tonight I told him I would raise my hand, and as the song ended, I will play a song wanted to see if they noticed.

I saw this bonehead go to the jukebox and put money in it; after a while, he went to the old man and told him the jukebox was broken, and he wanted his money back; the old man told him the jukebox as been turned off, the DJ is playing.

This stooge came up to me and said, "What are you going to do, I put money in the machine, and you cut it off." I told him, "I'll be a nice guy since it's early going; write down your songs, and I will play them for you." Now he started to get pissed at me, but he did give me a paper, and I looked and said, give me a minute, and I'll take care of you. I grabbed the mic and explained what I was doing, "This gentleman thought the jukebox was still on and did not notice the lights were shut off.

Einstein decided to put money into this machine turned off and didn't notice the sign that stated, the jukebox is shut off at 9 o'clock nightly. I told since I'm a nice guy, go make a list of the songs, and I will play them for you," so I played the first song, "Bon Jovi, Bad Machine; I heard someone yell, "Faggot." Then having a double, I'd play it again, a voice from the bar cried out, "That's not my songs, " I ask, "Are you sure because that's what it says on this paper you gave me (as I held up the paper), in fact here's your last song, it was another Bon Jovi song.

"WTF, stop fucking with me, jerk off," he yelled out. Now I had some guys coming over to the booth laughing their asses off and said, you are the man. After the song, I said, "Holy shit, I'm sorry that was the list from last night from these fabulous young ladies; here's your list," then I dropped the needle and played his songs. "Now, the next time before you put money in a jukebox, make sure the lights are on, you putz."

A Visitor To the Booth

To my surprise, she came to visit me tonight. The old man at the end of the night, started to call her my girlfriend and said, "Watch out, kid, you got the attention of some of these other shanks.

In the Groove

The old man was right as the other barflies saw me talking to her. They began to make their voyage to the DJ booth. Bones came up and said, "Watch out these sluts they get jealous fast in this place," and with that said, I thought to myself, don't eat where you shit.

I played on the microphone chopping the customers down n making the bar into a neighborhood bar where everyone knows the inside jokes. I can't believe they like being called assholes and verbally asphalted by someone on the microphone.

For example, I saw Bobby sitting at the bar bored, and I would call him out and say, "Hey Bob, what's wrong? You haven't heard Madonna in the last 2 hours; the bar would yell, "Faggot." Here you go, honey.

What Now

The old man came up to me as I was playing, and this wasn't good because he rarely talks to me during the night unless I go to the bar. He asks, "Do you have a problem with John?" I said no, but the old man said, "You haven't acknowledged him on the mic tonight." I usually start the night off by recognizing some of the regulars when I start the show. This guy usually sits there quiet and reserved; he stays away from the lights and attention. Now he wants to be part of the show; here you go, jerk off, I said, "What"? Okay, I'll take care of it." All of a sudden, I tap the needle SCREEEEEEEEACH....

"Pardon me for the interruption, but it was brought to my attention John "the Dobie Brother Reject" feelings were hurt since I did not say HELLO...Boohoo, I just started 25 minutes ago. I didn't know I had a time limit...so r u alright is there anything I can do for u since this rant is all about you (I went off for at least 3 minutes, and everyone was pissing their pants)? I can come over n suck your dick or get back to the regularly scheduled program." I dropped the needle, and John came over to buy me a drink and said he was sorry. He was laughing and said he was okay.

Tonight, DOMINO was born, I became the heartless son of a bitch the old man wanted or did he.

Excuse You...Your Talking About The Woman I Lust For

It's towards the end of the night at the Rock. I was making my way to the restroom; there she is. Bam, this guy turned to me and said, "I bet her pussy taste like pure candy."

What am I supposed to say, "Get back to me and let me know what flavor of a jolly rancher it was."? I'll never know.

In the Groove

I'd drove home from the bar and wondered why people like to be stripped down in a crowd. Do they have to LOOK AT ME SYNDROME? I don't know, but whatever it is, it's working, and I know I'm up to 4 nights a week.

Am I Ready For This

The apple of my attention has been going better, and I even got the nerve to ask her out to record shopping to help me out on some of the stuff to buy, but little did I know she had a son, and he was coming with us.

I'm in the store trying to concentrate on her while her son is running around like a lunatic. I thought to myself, I'm only 20, and am I ready for a premade family, but good damn, her body was screaming to me.

Back To School

I stopped over to Singers, and to my surprise, John and Brandy were there. I was talking to John and didn't realize we had a lot in common. He told me how Brandy and himself work on a college station, where does a mix show, and Brandy interviews recording artists. I told him I was working at a station as a production/producer part-time and spinning at the rock bar at nights.

He was surprised that I knew so much about dance and R&B music. I said, what? White boys aren't supposed to know dance music. He told Brandy, "I think we found our white son."

Sunday and Nothing To Do

My buddies came up, and I started to get friendly with some of the locals, and we talked aloud. Is there anything going on tonight? My buddy said, "We can go over to the pool I work at and crash it." It sounded like a plan, and to my surprise, she came along with us. Yes, the girl is hanging, but I'm a real pussy and can't get up the nerve to make a move on her.

We went to the pool club, and to our surprise, we had to jump the fence to get in. A couple of the guys started to do Mary Poppins off the high dive with the picnic umbrellas.

Before I knew it, I was thrown in the pool with her by one of the bartenders. We got out, but I wimped out and blew my move. I drove home that night, kicking myself, and promised that I would find courage when she gets back from vacation.

You're Hired

The boss pulled me aside tonight and told me the gig was mine because I do not have that dirtbag back here. I said sure.

I was embracing my new ultra-ego as a sexiest, womanizer, heartless son of a bitch; he only came out when the microphone was on, then back to the polite young boy my mother raised. The old man said we would do Thursday through Sunday during the summer.

Later, I was approached by this drunk and said, I hear you're with my girl; make sure you take care of them. Then he left, but she popped up and asks, "What did my ex want?" great, now I have to deal with this.

I Need a Closer

Now the gig is mine. I've played two songs as the closer: Frank Sinatra, New York, New York (when the old man was working, and The Curley Shuffle (for Jr.). The bar was torn between picking one song as the closer.

My Bodyguard

The bar was divided into two crowds, the before 8:30 crowd and the 9:00 crowd; the early birds are made up of drunks that liked their booze on the low down and after 9 group just wanted to party. I was approached by one of the early birds, Chink leaves, before I start playing. Chink told me that he couldn't stand the kids, but he likes me, and anytime I need him, he will be there.

Later that night, Chink was still hanging and was lit up like a Christmas tree. He was walking me back to the DJ booth, and all of a sudden, someone bumped me and said, "HEY ASSHOLE, WHEN ARE YOU GOING TO PLAY MY SONG." Chink told him to SHUT THE FUCK UP; the dude told Chink to go fuck himself, and before I knew it, the guy was laid out on the ground. I said to myself, I guess that's why they call Chink one punch.

Chink turned to me and said, "Welcome to the family, and I guess he won't bother you anymore tonight."

He Did What

I saw Chink when I came to the bar tonight and went over to say thanks for the other night. I saw tinsel on the bar next to him, and he asks, "want to see something."

All of a sudden, "I hear NOOOOO don't do it."

Chink lowered his head to the bar and snorted the tinsel; then, he jumped up, shaking his body and jumping up and down. I shook my head in disbelief. He said, "Are you sure you want to work here because we're all fucked up? WELCOME TO THE FAMILY; that shit hurts going down the nose."

It's Official. The old man got his song; we made it official tonight, New York, New York is the official closing song of the Rock.

There Goes My First Whip

Driving to work tonight, I saw the engine smoking and remembering the mechanic telling me I had six months before the car will burn up. I made it to the rock, and the early birds were laughing because the car was smoking, and lucky me, it was raining, so I opened the hood up to cool the engine off.

I sat at the bar and ask for the newspaper and said it's time for a new car, any suggestions? So it looks like I need a ride home tonight.

WTF...There's A What In My Car

The old man grabbed me and said, you have to give me a ride home with the new car I'm paying for. Shit...it's 3 a.m., and who the hell is calling me. I thought it was a bar fly, but worst it was the old man.

He said, go to your car and look under the seat its tonight's take; make sure it's there...GO NOW. There it was, a brown paper bag loaded with money and something else, to my surprise. I came back to the house and told the old man I got it and what the fuck do I do with your gun. He said to hide it from your mother and come into work by 10 a.m. to drop it off. I was walking up the stairs, and my mother asks what's going on, I told her I drove the old man home, and he left tonight's take in my car.

Do you Want A Ride?

The apple of my lust approached me; she asked, "Is that your new car." "Why do you want to go take a ride? I can see if I can steal the keys from the owner," I replied. We actually had a good conversation going, and now I'm in trouble; I made plans to go to the movies with her and her sister alongside my bubby, but now I have to clear it with Lou. I did take her home tonight but did not break in the new car.

Do You Have What?

Today I had a strange request; a guy came up and said, "I like your music, but you need to play more local bands."

I respond, "If you have them and if they fit the format, no problem." Then he asks, "Do you have a cassette player; I have some Ernie White live tapes?" Ernie is a big deal in the area and plays every Monday night at another bar. I told the kid I'd bring one in tomorrow.

"What A Dick"

I worked at the radio station today in the production studio for Don. Don always warned me about Larry and told me, "Don't let him push you around; everything he needs to be done is a rush." Just like Don said, here comes Larry, "I need the studio for 10 minutes, thanks." I figured let me get a smoke and come back without fighting with this duchebag. I came back and said, your time is up. I need to get these spots done before I leave.

I started to dub some spots, and the cd door opens and the head cleaner with the cap open poured across the remote board and fried that part of the board. I told the big boss that Larry was there and did not put the lid back on the head cleaner when asked what happened. I was told Larry would get spoken to and not to be afraid to throw him out of the studio next time. I found the DB got his ass reamed out, and the damage cost over three grand.

Hit The Record Button

Today, I was back at the radio station and was told I had to record the Rutgers men's soccer team show. I kept looking at the clock, and with every minute closer, I got nervous; it was the first time I would work with multiple people at once. The time finally came, and the hosts walked in asking if I was ready, let's do a soundcheck and then roll tape. I gave the sign, and about 30 minutes in, I noticed the red light blinking; WHAT THE FUCK, the first half wasn't being taped. Now I had to interrupt and tell them we had tech problems and need to start over. I didn't make any fans today, but we finally got it done.

Date Night

It's Monday, and Domino is going out to play, so I thought. I had to pay for his ticket and pick up any other foursome fees to get Lou to go. After I stopped into a WaWa and bought her some flowers, we went to the movies and gave me some brownie points, but Lou kept sucking the air out of any positive movement I had. Whatever, I suggested to do something else, and guess who shot it down? All I heard was I got to get up early tomorrow to work the pool. So, my so-called date was over next time; you know who stays home.

Thanks, Lou.

Surprise, Surprise

I got a visit to the DJ booth, and she said besides Lou, she had a good time, but next time can we leave Lou home.

Wrong Bar, Fag

It was a nice day driving into the Rock today. I had my windows down and blaring my "boom boom music." I looked in the parking lot and saw about four bikers from the Breed motorcycle gang (they were about 6 foot 3 and over 300 pounds each) give me the stare of death.

I pulled into my parking spot and was greeted by the nice gentleman, "Hey, the Granada is down the street, you disco

Joe walks out of the bar and asks the guys what's going on; they responded by telling him they were pointing me in the right direction. Joe said, "If you want music tonight, you better let him in." They shook their heads and said that we heard the new DJ play some mean tones, not this disco shit.

Joe replied, "Yea, but he's a little fuck up, but we love him anyway."

Why Can't She Say No?

I like this girl, but I can't stand her doing valium and other shit, especially while she's trying to raise her son alone.

I tell her all the time, but she says she needs relief from the pressures.

The Music Is Booming

Tonight, I got more compliments about the music, and my reply was, "That's what happens when you don't have to play requests all night long; it's my turn to pick them."

Duck, Incoming

Tonight, I experienced my first actual Rock throw down. The local dealer was in, and the funny thing was he had no real friends at the bar.

Suddenly, I am cueing up a record and look up and see this crowd coming towards the DJ booth with a bar stood held in the air heading inside the booth. WTF, the booth is like six by six and nowhere to hide; what to do? I put my hands in the glass opening to block any incoming. Next, I saw a buck knife coming my way. The crowd moved quickly across the room, and it was like a birthday possession where everyone was beating the shit out of this dude. I saw a couple of brass knucks and bar stools slamming him. He finally made it out of the bar into the cop's arms.

At the end of the night, Bones came up to me and asked, "You need a ride around the block after work."

I wondered what he met by that, but I soon to find out. They called him bones, and that's what we did, lit them up and unwind.

Light Up The Disco Ball

Hey, the disco boy had a bright idea. Why don't we add chase lights and a disco ball to the motif of the bar? Now, remember, the Rock is a hardcore rock and metal bar. I thought it would add to the music. Plus, the sound shop I go to gave me a great deal...free trial. I talked to the old man about it, and he said we could try it.

Let's Hang These Suckers

Today was the day to hang up the lights. I was getting comments like, "You're not turning this bar into a disco bar" or "When are the strippers starting."

What did I do? I'm feeling wrong about this decision, but tonight will be the test when they go on. I came back to the Rock and got into the booth on my way. Their customers were making comments about the new addition.

I blamed it on the old man and said he wanted to try something different. I finally felt like this was my bar, and I could contribute or shape it but not change the culture.

Here we go; Bon Jovi was an excellent cherry breaker, and how many girls lost their cherry during a Bon Jovi song. I decided to go with "You Give Love A Bad Name" because, besides the ladies digging him, it had significant kick parts for the chase floodlights. Here comes the break and cue the lights, Shot Through The Heart... the lights swept back in force, crisscrossing each other, and the bar went, "What the FUCK." The key to this madness is DO NOT OVERKILL THEM. I give the concert experience in their bar stool.

Hey, These Lights Are Better for The After Hours

It's been a couple of days since the lights debuted, and I've been receiving a good reputation as a hardcore R&R jock.

Now I have been getting some dancers coming in on their nights off to the party. After everyone left the bar, I went to the bathroom, and when I came out, three girls were sitting at the bar and Jr. (the old man's son) told me to put some music on, letting the girls shake their asses too.

All of a sudden, I saw the bartender and bouncer close the curtains. I looked over to the bar, and this girl was getting on top and yelled at me, "TURN THIS FUCKING SHIT OFF AND PLAY SOME GOOD SHIT." WTF? Here comes Bon Jovi, Bam, then the clothes started to come off. The lights were off, and my "disco lights" were the focus. Before we knew it, another one was on top of the bar giving one of the bartenders a private dance, and the third girl was on her knees with JR. I thought to myself, I don't particularly appreciate going to these places now I'm stuck at work with this situation. It's 2:30, and all I want to do is go home.

I Got Crabs Without Going To The Shore

Two days later, after the stripper-thon rumors have it, somebody got crabs from one of the fine ladies, and it wasn't me.

Hometown Bands

I've been taking the advice of playing more local and jersey bands besides Bon Jovi and Springsteen. I've been getting a lot of cassettes and names to buy.

Tonight, I got a surprise. One of the regulars asked if he can see the TT Qix record, and when he gave it back to me, he "said look at the cover." 2 out of the three were signed, Curt said, "They're my boys, and they're on a break from their tour and wanted to meet someone that supported local bands." I went over to say hi, and they were impressed that I was playing a lot of jersey bands and the other music. Like they say on the radio, you never know whose listening, now you never know whose sitting in the bar listening.

It's My Birthday

I finally turned 21 but couldn't tell anybody they thought I was older.

I told my mom don't do anything significant tonight. The old man came over to me before I started and said I heard it was your birthday. I told him my mom was coming in with a cake, and he replied, "Do you want me to like a jerk off, tell her to stay away." Now, the old man knew my mother for years and knew she doesn't play.

First, I looked up and saw her and six other people coming into the bar with a cake and balloons; the worst thing was I was smoking at the time. I ran out of the booth and told her she has to leave because the old man will fire me if you stay.

She went over to him, and the prick embraced her and said, what a beautiful thing you're doing. "I was going to do something over the weekend for him," the old man told her. What an ass. I had to act like a real jerk to my mom, and she even got a magician. The funny thing was I told him last week it was going to be my birthday.

Do You Notice The Crowd

I saw something different from the crowd tonight, so I went over to Mr. Personality, the bartender, and asked him I see an early Granada crowd, especially with these women.

Mr. Personality said, "They came in for the cheap ladies' night drink prices, and then when they go there, they buy one drink and there good." He continued and said, "I saw you keep it poppy, and they stood a little longer."

When they come on Friday, I told him I'll have them here longer, and I will blame my method on you. Mr. Personality said, "IF I get laid out of the deal, better yet.

Last Call

After my night was done, we went to the Granada for the last call. The Granada bartenders and manager would hang at the Rock on their days off, so we took care of each other.

LAST CALL...I'm sitting at the bar having a couple of drinks, and I asked Billy, "Where is Jeff?" Suddenly, Jeff came into the middle of 5 guys throwing punches as the bar was clearing out.

The bartender looked at us while laughing, "NO MATTER WHERE YOU ARE, YOU CAN"T TAKE THE ROCK OUT OF THE BOYS.

Let's See If The Method To My Madness Works

I saw the ladies parting down, and I flashed Mr. Personality, and he said, "Go for it." I did my usual introduction to a train wreck request but said, "It was going out to Mr. Personality because he's feeling neglected on tips, so I wanted to play one of his favorite songs Samantha Fox, I Wanda Have Some Fun, gentleman, and ladies he makes me play this every night after hours, it motivates him to clean up." Now the regulars were calling him a fag, but I saw a little bar stool jiggle going on, and I followed it up with Da Butt by EU. To my surprise, they got up, and people started dancing; the old man went nuts and had the doorman grab the tables out of the way. I keep the trend up with one more by Salt N Pepa; dam I had to go to the bathroom, and our makeshift dance floor was packed; on my way back to the booth, the big ass biker dude stopped me and said, "If I don't see that (he pointed to the girl's asses) I better not hear this (pointing to the speakers)."

I spoke to Mr. Personality after we closed, and he said I picked up a couple more bucks plus them bitches stood and extra hour; you nailed it with the perfect timing." The old man said, "You have balls playing that here, but it worked.

I'd Made It To November

It was a good night, and Thanksgiving is around the corner. I've become friendlier with the woman of a far but, chicken shit had opportunities but keeps pulling back when it's there. What an asshole I am. On a good note, the bar keeps breaking records every weekend; the bartenders and the old man is happy because their wallets are full. I heard a rumor that another night was going to be added soon.

Life is good.

You Almost Gave Me A Heart Attack

It was another jammed packed Friday, and the old man came up to me at the end of the night and said I almost killed him tonight; he continued and said, "Bill Jr. came by styling in a limo and had a hoe with him and had her take care of me. I ask, "What did I do?" He replied, "We went downstairs to the office, and she was sucking the shit out of me, and your fucking music was going BOOM BOOM BOOM (shaking the shit out of the ceiling and walls); between both of yous my heart felt like it was coming out of my chest.

The Best Night of The Year

Who would think the night before Thanksgiving was the best party night of the year? It was like a reunion of degenerates, college kids coming back home, the casual bar type, or the regular bar fly looking to get laid. That made it the best; everyone just wanted to get some and be merry, happy drunk night.

6 Months Already

I can't believe it's six months since I started this journey. I have to stop burning it up every night with Bones to unwind after the bar closes, feeling less stress. I still didn't get anywhere with her, but I'm starting to get rock star treatment from others, either getting pickup at the bar or someone waiting at my house. I can embrace this for a 21-year-old kid living the dream.

She'll Clean Your Pipes

The old man asks me after hours, "I saw you were talking to Bonnie, and you think she's in your league, she'll teach you a few tricks."

Plus, now, you have the queen of the bar's attention, and she'll be visiting you. I started getting my bar fly groupies, but I got this covered, blue balls all night long as a man of action.

Here Comes Another Contestant

Bonnie's girlfriend came up and introduced herself to me, and she was smoking; I would be all over that if I had the guts to walk through the door. She hung out with me in the booth, found out she was going out with a deadhead, but she flirted like crazy.

Bones came up to me and said, did you know she and Bonnie are bi and get it on together. Damn every man's dream, and it's on my front door.

Christmas Bonuses

It's about two weeks before Xmas, and the old man says I got a surprise for you, so tell them, whores, you bother with your busy after work. After the bar closed, I noticed a woman was sitting at the bar. The old man said Merry Christmas, "It's time you break in them both." Before I knew it, we were in the booth, and she was going down on me; I looked up and saw the rest of the crew looking on.

Now What?

It's Christmas Night, and nothing was going on; I should be happy I got the night off and get to relax. The boys and I are looking for something to do, so I called the Rock, and the old man answered. I asked if he was open, but he didn't know for how long.

We figured what the hell and took a road trip. We pulled in to the Rock, and there were cars in the parking lot for 8 o'clock on Xmas.

I ask the old man if we can put some music on, and he responded I'm not paying, I told him Merry Christmas; before you knew it, the bar was packed, and word spread that I was playing. It was a good night. We told them tonight's on me no FUCKING request. Tonight, I realized what a draw I am because some came up to me and said, if you weren't here, I'd be home, thank you.

What A Year!!!

Driving home tonight, I reflected on the past year and how much I accomplished in a short period. I started the year lost in direction and now establishing myself in the bar world as a respected DJ. It was funny just months ago; nobody paid me any attention when I walked into different bars, but now people yelling my name "Domino," buying me drinks, and approaching me as they knew me for years.

I have been stepping up my game with the woman and be more aggressive on the microphone.

I laugh at myself for how I am making so much money doing what I do? People are strange. It's scary knowing he was always in me, and now the beast is released between 8:30 to 1:30 Wednesday through Sunday; by the way, the old man added another night starting in January.

Hey Big Man

The old man approached me tonight and said, "HEY KID, REMEMBER I MADE YOU AND I CAN EARSE YOU." It was like a George Steinbrenner moment dressing down one of his players. I knew what he met...keep grounded, but he was afraid the notoriety would get to me.

Night Off

I went out with Bones and the boys to see Ernie White playing at Smitty Kicks (a so-called competition bar). I went to the back bar, and all I heard was, look at this, the Rock is here, but their bartenders always treated us right because they would hang at our bar on their night off.

We went to the front bar to hear Ernie, and after his set, Kevin approached him, "Hey Ernie, I want to introduce to someone. This is Domino." Ernie, to my surprised, knew of me and was very grateful for the local support. I suggested we should do something together on our off nights, and he said to keep me in touch. Monday nights is Ernie's big night around town, thank god, cause the old man would probably add another night.

Hey, Boss, I got an Idea

Before I started tonight, I pulled the Old Man over and told him about my encounter with Ernie; I said, what about on a Tuesday or Thursday night? We have Ernie and his band come in as guess DJ; give them an open bar with a cap on it. I was taken back because he agreed and said, see what dates will work, try to do it on a Tuesday.

Do You Know....?

I went inside the pit to get a drink, and the old man said, "Do you know these assholes sitting on the corner of the bar in front of the booth?"

I said, "Why should I," he replied, "They want your job, and you know I've been getting more calls by DJs lately for interviews, especially Tony Ninni. So, I asked, "Any of the contenders," he just pointed for me to get back in the booth with a big smile planted on his face. I know it's been a short time, but I became an animal. I don't give a fuck about these jerk-offs; they want mine to come and get it.

When I was starting and reached out to some of these asses for work, they hung the phone on me, especially Tony. I got back in the booth, wrenched it up a couple of notches, and called out the wannabes; I'd introduced them to the bar and said they wanted to bump me.

Before I knew it, the crowd started to chant, "Domino Domino, I jumped in WHOS HOUSE, and they responded DOMINOS HOUSE (I was having a RUN-DNC moment), I looked at the old man, and he shook his head like what did I create. I did ask them tryouts are tomorrow we should book you in, and then they got up and walked out.

After I got done and was sitting at the bar, the old man came over and said, where that came from? Why should I be any different, no matter who it is? I ask if he had a problem with that, and he said as long as these seats are packed every night, no problem. He did admit it was ballsy and quite funny.

Look What I Found

It's another Saturday night after hours, and when the old man works, he likes to do the foodie thing with Italian hoagies after hours. While the guys are cleaning up, I found a hot wheels car and started to push it around the bar, and the old man asks, "What are doing?" it's the newest thing hot wheels bar racing; he just laughed.

I'm Not Your Bitch For Drink or a Dollar

Tonight, someone tried to give me a buck to play his song; I said, "I'm not a fucking jukebox." If you take money or a drunk from these asses, they feel they owe you all night long.

I love it when they bring a drink up to me, especially if I don't know you, I will turn it down, and they look at you like your crazy. If they only knew what I was drinking, a simple juice mix, it looks like an Alabama Slammer.

The best tip (sarcasm) is when a bar fly comes up and grabs my monkey or flashes their tits; they think they get their songs faster. I like it when they return and say, "Where's my song? I reply, as soon as you finish me off, no down payments here.

You Are Throwing My Money Away

What's this? The old man is coming up to the booth with a bucket. He started to yell at me, "WHAT THE FUCK IS YOUR PROBLEM? IF THESE ASSHOLES WANT TO BUY YOU A DRINK, YOU TAKE IT."

I said, "What's up with the bucket" "THIS IS WHERE YOU POUR THE FUCKING DRINK THAT YOU DON'T; I WANT TO SEE THE BUCKET AT THE END OF THE NIGHT." I told the old man why I don't accept drinks and money for tips, he said, but now you're taking money out of my pocket, and off he went.

Now I'm Pissed

I was having a good night until that goddam record skipped. The place was packed, and they were letting me have it; I thought quickly, I have a double, so instead of this happing again, I grabbed the mic and said, "This is the last time, say goodbye."

There is a sharp corner in the front of the booth; I took the record and smacked on edge; it shattered all over the place, rock star fashion, the bar went crazy. Some idiots ran over to grab the pieces for a keepsake, and some stood in morning of a broken album.

Another Sunday Night

Sunday nights are usually deficient; the crowd usually doesn't bother me and let me play what I want (no requests needed); Lou came up tonight, which is usually trouble. We got bored, and I challenged him to a game of one up. The rules are simple, I play a song, and you match it either in the same genre or not; if you want to change the mood, pop a slow song. If we are in a groove, this can go on for hours, making great cassettes.

We usually do this in the basement; it's a great exercise to know your music and learn how to jump from mental to pop to classic rock to southern rock.

Visitor's Day

The more I'd played unapproachably, these pigs would play with me more, and it was like a challenge, who's going to tap the DJ first.

Bonnie came up and invited me to come over after the bar closes for a bit of party. I was nervous but said sure. I called the last call and grabbed two six-packs, and off I went.

I got to her house, and as soon as I got in, I realized I locked my keys in the car; someone gave me a ride to my house for my spare set. I got back, and a majority of the crowd was gone, and when we were left alone, she was lying down across the room stroking herself with her legs spread just enough to give me an invite, but this guy goes, what time is your boyfriend picking you up Florida in the morning, there goes the mood dummy.

Here Comes The Other One

Bonnie's girl Vikki comes in tonight and hangs in the booth for a while, trying to allure me, goddam did she smell good, and those pantyhose she wears makes you want to rip them apart. She asked if I was available to hang after work, and I invited her over for breakfast; she was surprised. I couldn't wait to get out of here.

The old man grabbed me and said, the other one is out of town, so; you're going to try this one. She followed me in her car, and we relaxed a little, then I made her some eggs. I got her into the other room, and I went forward this time. I did the yellow pages and let my finger do the walking, she exploded and started to cry, and she said she has to see her boyfriend then ran out of the house. I followed her to her car and noticed her silk pantyhose were worn to shreds; I thought, good luck explaining that one.

The Skanks Know

It was a regular jammed-packed Friday night, except there was blood in the water. These sharks were extra flirty tonight.

I was getting it from every direction. I broke my golden rule, and now I have to pay for it. The old man enjoyed himself as they were one-upping each other; they wouldn't ask to come into the booth. They just walked in at one time. There were 4 of them and me. I had to go to the bathroom to get out, and when I came back, I made sure that the door was locked.

One female I wish that would leave me alone was her. She was zonked, and I said, "Don't talk to me when you're like this.

Let's Get Out Of Here

She pissed me off tonight. I can tell she was on something and was glad she left early. The boys wanted to go over to the Granada for the last call, and I was in. The only bad news I heard she was going to be over there; WTF? She never goes there cause of the people and music. I noticed it was snowing pretty good, but what the hell? We went, and the old man told me, "You going to see your girlfriend," I laughed and said, "Fuck her."

We got to the Granada and went to our corner bar and of course, who is there? I told her to leave me alone, but she was all nice, rubbing up on me. It was time to go, and her girlfriend came over, a real bitch and cousin to the old man and wouldn't let me forget it.

Jeff talked me into giving them a ride home that night, I probably would have nailed it, but she was pissing me off.

I'd told them if they say one fucking word, I will pull over and out you go. We pull out of the parking lot, and her girlfriend started on me. I stopped the car and said, "If you don't shut the fuck up, your walking, and I don't care how bad it is outside" (SILENCE); for a second, then that bitch opened her mouth, I said, "Lucky the Rock is down the street I'll drop your asses off there, and you can use the payphone outside the bar.

I came back and went inside the bar, and the old man asks, "What happen? I see your girlfriend outside," All of a sudden, they were knocking on the door; the old man said, "Should I let them in." I responded, "FUCK her and your cousin." He was shocked, and he asks, but it's like a blizzard outside; I replied, "I was nice. I could have dropped them off in the middle of the street; I'm done." He then came over and gave me a draft and said that you got some guts with these bitches tonight.

What Does He Want?

I'd picked up the phone and heard that voice, broken English, jerk off, "Hey Dom, it's Tony Ninni; I want to talk to you." He continued, "I hear you are lighting the rock world on its tail, I wanted to expand into the rock scene and want you to turn over the Rock to me, and you can be in charge of my rock division."

"Are you fucking serious? Five years ago, you didn't want to know my name, now you want me, I heard you called the old man, and he told you to call someone else," I responded. I'm surprised he still had my number anyway. I think he got my answer.

Tony inquired if one of his guys can come down and hang with me to see the master. I've must have been sick in the head but said yes.

You Did What?

I came into work and told the old man, guess who I got a call from yesterday. He replied, "Tony Ninni, I told him I got a DJ. I don't need you." I told the old man do you want to laugh? He wants one of his guys to hang with me. He replied, "I hope you told him to go fuck himself," No, I said, come on down. The old man said, "I created a monster."

I am different from when I first entered the Rock; now, if you want it, come and get it. There is only one Domino, and no one can duplicate him, thank god, I don't think the world can take two.

Radio Star

I can't believe I am balancing the bar and the radio station; they have been giving me more hours at the station. I've been coming a long way; I think my confidence is beginning to build up to embrace what I do.

Today I met Tony D, and he was telling me some of his experiences in radio. He told me about the first day at this radio station (he was doing the morning show on a Saturday); he looked around the station and could not find anyone; he looked into the studio, saw the on-air light go on and an arm coming up and grabbing the mic and pulling it down.

Tony then said, "He saw the jock with some girl underneath the board as he was doing his show, he was doing her," he added, "Only in radio kid."

A Singer Calls Me

Hot Traxx calls me tonight and wanted to see if I wanted to join him and Brandy next Tuesday night to go to "Dancing On Air." They were going to interview Timmy T; I thought it would be someone big like Madonna, Will Smith, or The Jets,...Timmy T, this guy's career was built on his ex-girlfriend breaking upon him. I said, what the hell? It should be fun.

We got there, and Brandy asks me, do you know who this guy is. I replied, "That's why you brought the white guy with you." We sat down, Timmy came in, and I started talking to him and building up, saying I play your song all the time (I did have it, but the plastic was still sealed), I dropped some info out there, and lucky someone was listening.

Brandy did her interview, and Timmy was very impressed with how prepared she was, and it was his pleasure. Hey, girl, the only thing you knew was his name. Hot Traxx told me we have to hang more.

Hey Rock Star

Today was an interesting night off for a Monday, and off we went to Kicks to see the legend, Ernie. I walked in and got, "Here goes the neighborhood; the Rock is here."

Then I hear my name over the sound system, and it was Ernie, giving me respect for supporting the local scene.

I felt like a rock star; it felt weird when I walk into different bars and hear my name. I grabbed Ernie when his set was done and said I talked to the old man, and he said it's a go, bring the whole band, drinks, of course, is on him to a point, and we will jam in my house. He said, "This should be sweet, me the DJ."

We settled for a Tuesday when we have nothing going on, so the old man got me free and Ernie and his band in on an off night.

It's Fun Time With The Wannabe

It's been a slow week for a change, and tonight is what I needed to break up the boredom. Toni's wannabe came in to see what the hype is all about. This kid was like me. He preferred dance but knew rock music.

So, I went over my philosophy and how I flow all these styles together like your mixing dance music. His head looked like it was exploding; I was in a groove talking to him, but being the showman, Domino came out, and he just shook his head.

I told him, "I don't mix. I'm a party jock, but I can blend the Rock, (I got a look like what the hell is talking about)," I was playing a song that ended cold with a fade and brought in Aldo Nova, Fantasy, (it has such a long-ass intro I would bring it to the kick), and it would blend without the bullshit.

He just shook his head and said, WTF, I've seen enough; I'll let Tony know.

The Reviews Are Out

Tony called me tonight and ask, "When do we get this done and take over the rock world." He continued, "My boy said you know how to work a crowd, please everybody with multiple genres, and he never saw someone read a crowd the way you do." I like this. Tony is kissing my ass; usually, he's the one with your tongue shoved up his ass. He added I couldn't teach Domino, so I want Domino to be a part of my empire. I told this duchebag, "5 years ago, you had the opportunity to get on the ground floor of Domino, now Domino doesn't need you or any other organization, so you can just go fuck yourself." By the way, that means NO.

I did learn something from that conversation, and I thought every jock had these skill sets but was relieved only a few possessed them. I always felt a surge of energy from the room when I played and noticed I could bring it up or down at a moment's notice, but I thought that was done by picking the right song; I was wrong; what I do, you can't teach. Wow, I got the power.

The Phone Rang

Tonight, I was getting ready to go to the bar. The phone rang. To my surprise, it was her, and she was very apologetic about the other night. She did admit she has to slow down. She also said, "Can I say hi tonight if I come up." I always have a soft spot for her. The funny thing is we act like a married couple but never kissed yet.

Gentleman Start Your Engines

Tonight, Lou was hanging after hours and brought in a hot wheels car, and we were racing as the crew was cleaning.

The old man said, "You guys are fucked up." I said, "Football season is over, and nothing else is going on a Sunday afternoon; what do you have to lose." Lou added, "I'll do sound effects." I said the one thing the old man wouldn't turn down; it will be freebee. He agreed, and now Sunday Sunday Sunday is the Buffstone 500.

Hype the Hype

I started to hype the hot wheels races, and the joint went nuts; what kind of drugs are you on after a hour to I this you will love NASCAR. This will be fun. I started to give out hot wheels cars to promote the event.

Practice, Practice, Practice

Jr. was working tonight, and the bar had open space on the track, so I took my cars out to promote the race to the early crowd. They were laughing at me and said how hard it was to push a car around the bar. I would give my car to the naysayers, and they couldn't get it to go 5 feet. I took the car, and it went three-quarters around the bar before it hit a mug of beer. Now, they were hooked; it's like a carvel game; show them once, and now they have to do it.

It's Race Day

Holy Shit, the bar was filled (the bar was a vast oval and sat at least 70 people). The old man looked at me and said, it's your show. We had the bar mic on the floor, and Lou ran the sound from the booth.

The rules were simple; it was a buck a car, and you would get three tries for the distance. The farthest would be marked, and the top three would split the pot.

We had about 20 people participating, and some had multiple cars. Lou was playing theme songs and crash sounds as the cars would fly over the bar. The event took about 2 hours, and it was a blast, especially for me. I walked away with 40 bucks and the title of champion.

The old man was happy; he sold hot dogs and hamburgers, and the beer was flowing. We decided to do this for the next five weeks, and the Buffstone 500 was born.

I Got A Indecent Proposal

The old man came over to me and said, the queen wants to take you to the Satellite (it was a bar down by the military bases and was open until 5 in the morning) after your done. He talked to her last night and said, you are her mission tonight; he just wanted to give me a heads up. I said, "Thanks." I knew her from the neighborhood and knew very well of her reputation; she was all women and knew how to please.

Oh no, here she comes, she pointed to the door, and she walked in the booth and said, "I heard you are available tonight for the Satellite, be ready after you call, last call" (she started to grind me and out she went.)

Bones came over and said, "Better you than mean, here you're going to need this trust me (it was a condom)."

She came to the booth and said, we will meet you in the car, so hurry up. I was walking out, and the old man grabbed me and said, "Kid, you're going to get the best blowjob of your life; I'm jealous." I saw her partner in crime was in the backseat, and off we went.

I heard the band was good, and the third wheel knew the roadies and was hanging with them in the dressing room; we were drinking, and after a while, she said, "Let's go." We got back to my car, and she said, "I don't feel good and have to end this."

We lived down the street from each other, so I told her, do you want me to follow you home, and she said, "No, I'll be alright."

I saw her pull over and was throwing up outside the car. I was lucky because better on the street than in my lap, I thought to myself.

Did I Get Lucky

I walked into the bar tonight, and the old man came right over to me, like we were in high school, and ask what happen. I told him, "Absolutely NOTHING, (he looked like what did you do) she puked right after she dropped me off at my car. The old man said, laughing, "Only you."

Another Main Event

We finally settled on a date with Ernie so the whole band could be there.

So, it's time to promote the guest DJ next Tuesday night; Ernie White will be playing your favorites. The bar said where he would play here, I responded he would be spinning records, and the rest of the band will be here. Now Tuesday nights are dead, so it was a perfect night to do this because Ernie has a friendly draw.

It's Show Time

Tonight's the night, the bar was packed, and we knew it was going to be crazy, and of course, it's after 9 o'clock and no Ernie, the old man is going wild, all of a sudden I saw hair coming to the booth, and it was Ernie. I said, "Welcome to my house; what are we drinking." He introduced his group and said I don't know if Kenny (the drummer) is coming, maybe later. I gave a quick tour of the booth and asked if you want to call out by artist or prefer to dive in.

The records are divided up by category in alphabetical order. Ernie looked at me and said, "You weren't kidding about me playing." "Come on, rock star; it's easy; I'll show you," I told him. He added, "Well, my mother always wanted to find another skill if the music thing doesn't work out."

He got into the groove and was taking turns with the rest of the band all night. I had a surprise for him (I'd picked up a couple of his albums for a giveaway); I ask, "Do you know this song'" he laughed and grabbed the mic, and started to sing along with the album. The crowd went crazy, and then I said I have a problem; what are we going to do with these (I found out when I bought them they were the last of them in the area); he was shocked and called the band over, grabbed the sharpie. First, he and the band signed them, and then we gave them away.

Tonight was a blast, and I could believe they hung almost all night. It felt like another rock star night for me. The old man came over to me after it was over, and he said it was a good idea; I turned to him and said, "YOU going to pay me now."

I Can't Believe We Lasted This Long

We wrapped up the inaugural season of the Buffstone 500, and people were pissed cause I went undefeated and cashed in nicely.

Each week the pot got bigger and bigger because they wanted to knock off the champ. I won nearly 400 hundred bucks for the season.

Who Are You

Joey came in the bar tonight, now this isn't Joey's scene, but he came in with someone else, Gary. We hung, and Gary was telling how much he wanted to learn how to spin. Shit, here we go again, another wannabe.

It's Getting Close To My Anniversary

I can't believe my first anniversary was coming up, and I ask the old man what he would do for me. "I fucking pay you, isn't that enough, we will have a party, and I'll even put an ad in the paper." I was in shock because I remember what happened on my birthday.

Gary has been coming around and stopped in tonight; the only thing with this dude is he wants to bang everything in a skirt; the problem is, he is married.

The strange thing is the old man likes him; no wonder a pig likes a pig.

Road Trip

The crew at the Rock has been talking about taking a mobile party; we rent a limo and pick a direction.

Tonight, was insane. We decided to go to New York with my boys Joey and Lou, and from the Rock, Mr. Personality, and Big C, the bartenders, I loaded the bar up, and it was a constant party. I think the only time we got out was to piss.

We were driving around Times Square, and the boys noticed these beautiful ladies, so being an ass, I rolled the window down and called them over with a wave of the hand. Holy Shit, before we knew it, there were 3 of them jumping in the limo; now I did it.

We drove around, and they kept wanting to negotiate prices (what did you think they were); finally, we pulled over and had a conference; before we knew it, this bitch jump out of the car and started taking a piss behind the limo. Mr. Personality had a bright idea. He saw her pocketbook and kicked it under the car. She was looking for it, and our polite driver said, here it is. I guess that was better than stealing from her pimp.

So, the Whitney Houston wannabe said, so are we on, Mr. Personality, Big C, and I went back in, and the party was on; these girls were tired of waiting. The funny thing Mr. Personality kept going bareback, and his girl kept saying, "come on, white boy, keep it capped." After the fourth time, she said, ok, fuck me.

Later, I was told that Lou, Joe, and the driver were sitting on the limo because it bounced like a bronco bull. Joe told me he was getting air.

After we finished, they left, and we headed back home, but on the way back, Mr. Personality grabbed Big C's shoe and threw it out of the sunroof, thinking the sunroof was closed. Big C turned around and threw the other one out, and said, "What the hell? There goes $400.00 out the window."

Yes, $400.00, who knew a bartender at a rock bar, would style an Italian designer—what a night.

Recap

The first night back that since our trip to the city. I ask Tom if I knew a good spot to find an expensive Italian pair of shoes cheap, he responded, "Between exits 10 and 9 on the N.J. turnpike." Big C, turnaround from the bar and gave me the finger. The old man asks Mr. Personality, "What happened?" Mr. Personality told him, and the old man replied, "That's why I go to Payless."

During the night, I kept reminding Mr. Personality to put his hat on, and he would yell, "FUCK YOU." I kept the night low-key but kept it to insider humor to keep our lovely reputations outstanding in the community of dirtbags.

What Do They Want

I was approached by some of the local females that spoke to me on a minimal basis, and they told me, "Tony Ninni was organizing a D.J. awards show for the summer to honor the bar, club, and wedding jocks in Mercer County.

They ask if these categories fitted me, "Rock Jock, Party Jock, M.C., and Best Overall Jock." I said I'm honor, but he won't like seeing my name on the ballot."

Metal Heads Against the Deadheads

I did not want to hear Dead tonight, and the metalheads drove me crazy, so I decided to play a little game with them.

I pulled a Dead and Def Leppard album out and placed them on the ledge on the booth's front. The rules were simple; anybody asks for either one, the album would be handed other and destroy by the other party.

We made it through the night without any casualties, and the bar was upset, so I grabbed the albums and gave them to the opposing sides for destruction. It was in true fashion of the Buffstone; the metalhead's method was to smack it over one metal heads, and the dead heads choose to eat to an album; they passed it back and forth, taking a bite. I was told never to do this again since the deadhead was bleeding by eating the record.

The Summer Wind

It has been a mellow summer, but I have been thinking it's been a year working five nights, and it is starting to take a toll. I like the bar scene, but sometimes playing the same music for the same people night after night is annoying. My best night is when requests are at a manual. I like breaking new music or highlighting other songs on the album besides the releases.

I took a drive to Singers tonight and talked to him about doing radio on a full-term basis, and he said he would keep an ear out. I was currently working more hours in production, which I'm enjoying, but there is no advancement. Because of working at the bar, my hours will be selective, I was asked to work nights at the station, but I didn't want to give up the bar thing yet.

Bill said, "One day, you will have to decide whether it's radio full time or the bar business, but I do have something for you now; the Flemington fair is coming up, and I can use some announcers to promote events and vendors during the night." I'm not a mouthpiece, but this gig sounded like fun.

What Time Is It?

I needed a Saturday night off and decided to see Morris Day and Luther at the vet. Stupid me pick these two barflies that had no interest in me but embarking on a free ride. Of course, they were the apple of my distant eye. I had a buddy of mine fill in for me tonight, which was scary because he does this as a hobby, but he was known around the township because of his speed shop.

Of course, I had the limo; how else would one travel. The girls were shocked when I picked them up. The concert rocked, and I had a decent time with them for the most part. We came back to the Rock, and this was when the party started; Kenny and his boys (my D.J. fill in) ask him I still had the limo, and we decided to rent it out for the rest of the night. Keep in mind I started at 11 am, and now it's 1:00 am; the driver called it in and cleared it with the boss.

"Yoooooo, Domino." we were cruising around Seaside Heights, and I did my usual having my wrist outside the window, I heard. I looked but didn't see where it was coming from. The driver told us her girlfriend was having a party in Bel Mar, and we decided to go.

We got back by 6 in the morning and didn't want to see that bill; I was glad I paid for my portion before d round two started.

He's Out

When I came into work tonight, the old man asks if I had a good time the other night.

I said it was very interesting, and he said, "Good because that's your last in a long time if you have that goofball fill in for you." I screwed myself where I set the bar and have anybody work here; they have to be better than me.

I got comfortable here, and the customer felt the same way; they accepted my approach on the mic, and when someone didn't live up to those explanations, they were dead. I tell other jocks anybody can put music on a turntable, but a few can control the crowd.

In my bar, these fine upstanding citizens are coming in for a good time and relaxing. My job is to deliver every night and not think I'm playing in my bedroom.

I hate when jocks think they know the crowd and want to push their music down their throats. I can sneak in new music by camouflaging it around familiar songs the group knows, and then once in a while; you hear what that song before April Wine was."

I learned during my time here spinning; I realized it's more than throwing down records; it is a science, and it works. I developed my circle, and it keeps the bar going.

It's My Birthday

The old man made up for last year's fiasco and did nothing. My mom told me she was staying away this year, and the old man did nothing. This starts making me think all the fucking money I make this S.O.B., and he can't recognize me; where's the loyalty.

The boys didn't let me down, and Bones suggested that we take a limo trip to the city; we got the plans set, and off we will go.

It was funny later. Bones came back to the bar with a cake for me, and the old man said, "Whose birthday is it?"

It's Party Time

The limo was loaded, and I mean loaded when it comes to Bones and Flynn. Joey and Lou came to, and we promised no strangers to join in tonight. Our favorite driver was on tonight, and this guy is a trip; he can't drive over a bridge, so when we reach his height, he stops, and someone volunteers to push it down the peek. It was my birthday, and I wanted to do it, but Lou carried on like a little girl, so I conceded.

Suddenly, we hear a LOUD HORN and bright lights coming in fast; I grabbed my beer and downed it like it was my last; Bones and Flynn were puffing down their joint. Joey yelled, "Hey ASSHOLE, next time, look before you pull the hell out, jerk off." Lou came back to the back, and we all said collectively he's not driving on the way back.

We made it to McSorley's, this was Lou's favorite bar in the village, and it had cheap drafts. They give you an hour's time limit and then kick you out, especially if you sit at the table. The strange thing is they only had one bathroom, and you had to share at the same time with the ladies.

We cruised around the city and stopped at the Hard Rock for some burgers and beer.

It was a mellow but relaxing night away from the Rock; I did get a page from her wishing me a good time on my night with the boys. We headed out, and we were tanked. Thank god Lou passed out, and I couldn't walk to the front of the car, but I got it over the hump, and we resumed our journey back home safe.

I Was Picking Up Some Steam

Bibs (the Granada manager) approached me tonight and said, "He was looking in on adding a rock night either on a Tuesday or Sunday night and would like to have me take it over if it's alright with the old man." I was honored just to be asking because that joint was one of the hottest clubs in town. It's a nice stroke to one's ego when someone from the outside looks at you as a commodity.

I Get A Lecture Tonight

The old man must have gotten an extra shot of machismo tonight; after the bar was closed, he started giving me a tongue lashing on how I'm taking advantage of all these skirts that come in.

"Back in the day, me and your father were banging all of these whores, and your nothing like your father; you would be an embarrassment," the old man added.

That pissed me off because, for years, I suspected him of cheating on my mother but never got the truth until now.

I responded, "That was the nicest compliment somebody could give me, I never want to be like that man, and by the way, at least I know how to swim."

The old man went ballistic because the swimming remark referred back to old family secrets, and only close people knew the secret.

"Hey kid, I think you better get the fuck out of here...before anything else is said," the old man stated. I left feeling good. I stood up to him, and on the other hand, I wondered if I had a job.

They Said No

I asked him what's going on about rock night. "These prima donnas I have got their panties twisted and said they would leave if I came into their domain; the only one that spoke highly about you was Tony D.," Bibs explained to me.

I figured those cunts had their inner circle and looked at the bar jocks as a lower ring on the DJ food chain. The problem is those jacks could stand in my shoes for one hour at the Rock or any other bar.

I saw Tony and went over to the booth to thank him. "He said, "I ignore these jerk-offs are jealous of anybody to come into their domain."

My Favorite Time Of The Year

I saw her tonight; it has been a while, and I got another surprise. It was the night before Thanksgiving, and the question of the night was, "Are you going to do Christmas night?" I responded it depends on the old man.

The night before always brings out strangers of the past, and I got a pleasant surprise after work. After work, I went home but saw a car follow me; I thought it was a jerk off from the bar.

I got into my house and saw this I-Roc just staying in the middle of the street. So being a dummy, I went outside to see what the issue was at 2:30 in the morning.

As I approached the car, the window went down, and I heard, "Hey baby want to go for a ride?" It was this girl I use to hang with, but she hasn't been around in a long time, so I figured it's the season of giving, so I gave in. Before I knew it, we were in Trenton at the marine watching the submarine races.

Yes, I Know You're a DJ

Tonight, I had it. I hate when DJs say, hey, it's Dj blowjob, yes we know you're a DJ; the first clue is a microphone, and the seconds those two round things that make music out of them.

Some ass came over to me and said, "Hey, DJ Domino, play me a song."

I took to the mic venting my pet peeve and saying, are we that stupid that the jerk off behind the booth has to remind us that he is a DJ? Look at me, look at me, I'm the one playing the garbage you hear on the speakers or is it to remind themselves of their job and to stroke their ego. Christ, if anybody catches me saying that, just shot me. The crowd was getting into this, and I guess I'm like Madonna, where I can be Domino.

It's Race Time

I can't believe it's time for the second season of the Buffstone 200 hot wheels edition. This year everyone was coming after me, and all I wanted to do was lap the bar.

BayBay (bartender) told me my time was over, and I just said, bring it. I was surprised the bar was jammed, and Lou was back on the sound effects.

The rules were simple that there could be no physical or mechanical adjustments, or you will disqualify. The only thing you can do is adjust the tires.

I go to Toys r Us and pick my cars; on the meet day, I open the box and go. Some of these guys have been bringing cars to the bar ever since they heard we were bringing it back.

Here We Go Again

BayBay told me before the race today, "Your reign ends now."

I just laughed. I do this for fun. Some people are talking like it counts for something; oh yeah, the money isn't bad either.

BayBay got his dream and beat me today, but I placed second and third; he was gushing like a little girl after taking her virginity away. The old man was happy. Now he can bust my balls all week.

It's Foggy

I've been noticing that this week BayBay is working; he pulls out his cars at the end of the night, and I told him the more you use them, the more damage you can cause. He replied, "What I do to these cars it only improved them and pulled out a bag and said this is the magic gas." I am just amazed how serious some people need to win will do anything.

I ask him if you think he can beat me, get a car in a box and let's go because now a fun event is turning into a shame.

Anyway, today she came up and was very pleasant and told me all she is doing is her drink and, of course, some smoke. I said, well, no more junk. Later she asked me if she could have a ride home, and as we were driving, it was like a thick soup; you couldn't see shit in front of you. We got to her house, and she asks if I mind as she lit up a joint, I noticed her pants were undone, and she said I'm home and getting comfortable; we hung for an while, and I reached a little contact high (actually she shotgunned me). I told her I got to go, but she asks since the roads are bad do you want to sleep over and being the man I am? I was off into the fog.

The End of An Empire

I'd told the old man today was my last race, and I was done with this joke; he knew the kid was cheating for the past four weeks, and he just enjoyed me losing. It sucked not winning, but I was breaking records of mine and still making nice coins.

BayBay would never take me up on my offer. I challenged BayBay to an open box race, we both enter three brand new cars and open each one before we race (no prep time except for the three trails), and he would not take the challenge.

Every time you do something fun and different, some asshole has to ruin it for the masses. It was fun while it lasted, and the funny thing was I heard a couple of other bars heard about this and was doing the same; thank god they were a long drive down the road, but it was flattering; a stupid idea bloomed into two years of entertainment.

I'm Starting to Think Hard

I stopped by Singers before I went to work tonight, and Singer told me WHWH is looking for a full-time board operator, but it's overnights. I said I'll think about it. Singer gave me the number and said, "Call them and talk, then decide what you want to do."

The Phone Call

I went into work tonight, scared like a little bitch facing the old man. I got the phone call to change my life; the PD from WHWH, Ed, called me to offer me the job. I ask, "Can you give me a day because I have to work it out with my current employer." I explained my situation, and he was getting pissed, but I said I could have Gary take 11 pm to close on Thursday and Friday nights, and I will be here for Saturday nights, but Gary will also do Wednesday nights. I was surprised that he agreed; I guess he felt I would get them drunk enough; it would matter who finished.

In One

BOOTH IN
ANOTHER

I Must Be Crazy

Tonight, started my marathon, playing at the Rock until 11:00 and then drive down to the station. I was knocked out when I got home. I got to get used to these overnights. The crazy thing is I'm still working at the other station too.

Did I Make The Right Decision?

I was reflecting tonight, I like the station, and it was sweet that nobody is around to micromanage at the radio station.

On the other hand, the only thing is it's about a month in, and it's starting to take its toll, especially on the weekends.

Tonight, I brought in a six-pack, and we kept it outside, lucky for the snow to refrigerate it for us. The FM jock was incredible, and on Friday night, we started to have a beer around 3 am when we knew nobody was coming in unless they were invited.

Who's The Doctor?

For three months, I frequently hear about this doctor around three-ish in the morning. I finally met him, or should I say her, Mary Jane.

I also talked to the old man and said I couldn't do this anymore. It breaks me down, worrying about the bar and concentrating on my position at the station. I was surprised he said, "I'll have someone in next week. I told you they call me all the time." Boy was that I shot to the ego; I was that replaceable.

He also added, "This kid just called me today and said he has CDs and the modern equipment; maybe I'll give him the shot.

My Send-Off

My last night at the Rock was freezing when I walked by the old man; he just said, when can you get your stuff out so the new kid can set up. I didn't expect a party, but at least thanks for the boost in business.

This young kid walked up to me and said I am the new DJ, all I thought was they would eat this kid up; he's worse than when I started.

Radio Groupies on The AM

Tonight, the FM groupie decided to call me, and we would have some with her strange—the best thing about working at a radio station is you have many devices on hand. The jock from FM came over and thought I had hard punched up through the board.

This chick loved to give phone sex to whoever was on the phone. I had to take her out of cue to do commercials.

When I came back, I must have hit the wrong button because out of the speakers arrived, 'I want to suck your dick." Thank god for the delay, and nobody listens at 3 in the morning.

WTF I'm Not Your Delivery Service

The worst part of this position at the station is working with the morning jock; he thinks my job is to go out and get him breakfast, WTF, he drives in, and he can't stop in on the way in. I've started this shit because I agreed to it when I started, but this shit is getting old.

Today I told him, "This is my last time; start getting it before you roll in."

I Did What?

    I got a call this morning from my boss, and he wanted to know why my production is all screwed up; the tones are too early, the spot cuts off during the middle, or the cart is blank; I said, "What, I reply these spots over to make sure there is no problem." He suggested I keep doing that, and I know your production is usually flawless.

Is This Going To Be A Habit

What is going on? The boss called again and said, "What is going on? Are you getting sloppy on your production? Johnnie (the big boss heard it over the air and got pissed), the morning host, was also complaining to him about the quality of the spots. "I replied, "I don't understand; I've been double-checking it and having FM check the spot in their players. wait for a second, that SOB this has been happening ever since I stopped delivering Big Mike breakfast after my shift"

Ed came back with. First, he can get his breakfast on the way in; the second, I will give you some production, but make me a third copy and put it on my desk so that I can prove someone tampering with your production.

How stupid can one be because from 6 am until 8 am, there are only four people in the station? I hope this works.

The Rat Was In The Trap

What a dummy, he did it again, and my boss double-checked with his copy and found it clean, he went to his boss with the info, and he was going to get along talking too. He also added, "Mission complete, and he will not ask anyone for breakfast again.

Keep up the excellent work, and I'm glad we fixed the issue, have a good weekend."

Somebody Wasn't Happy This Morning

Big Dummy comes in the studio this morning, and I ask him, "Are there any issues with the production these days?" All I got was, "Fuck you."

I Need Direction

I went to Singers before I went to work and ask for direction since he got me the job there. I told him I've been for over six months, but I am going nowhere; I do more at CTC as a part-timer than at WHWH full time. I was told the big boss doesn't want me to work at CTC because of their competitors.

I feel like I'm wasting my time there. Singer told me, "Talk to your PD at CTC and explain your situation and ride it out; if it still gets worst quiet, you will always have the other station.

I noticed some new faces, and this one guy in particular stuck out (he looked like a Mickey Dolan wannabe), but he was cool as hell, we talked for a while, and he told me he joked and was working at a local TV station doing edits.

How Can I Explain This?

I was working at CTC, and it was the 4th of July; later, they would do the simulcast of the fireworks at the park with the world-famous Grucci Family. I told my PD to remember; I cannot be on the air.

Later, he got a call from my replacement and said he was not coming in, and I had Tony do all the vocal throw overs for the day until the fireworks.

It's getting time for fireworks, and Houston, we have a problem; the feed to go back to the Grucci's is not working; only I can hear them. The show must go on, and all I'm thinking about is I can't go on air because this is the biggest show in central jersey and who knows who's there.
Anyway, we made a line of callers barking out the cues to fire the fireworks. I thought they just fired, and it went bam.

There must have been over 500 calls, and my tongue was getting twisted. After the last call, all I heard was, "You are now an honorary Grucci, and applause followed. I worked my tail off, and after the 20-minute show, I felt I ran five marathons.
Once I got into regular programming, my PD called and said an excellent job. It was linked perfectly, and I told him we had problems with the feed, and he responded, " You could never tell and guess who I saw

at the park. "No shit," I said; he said he was thinking about going (it was my boss from the other station). I was just glad this day was overall 13 hours of it.

Guess Where I Went This Weekend?

I was finishing my shift at WH, and my boss came walking into the studio (filling in for his highness), said to me that he was at the fireworks show, and said he was very impressed and how the show seamlessly with the fireworks music.

He continued; your old station did a great job". Little did he know, as I was walking out of the studio, he asks, "Can you get me a bagel? Then started to laugh."

Is This My Way Out?

Tonight, I heard through the inside grapevine that the old man wasn't happy with my replacement, so I figured let's see if he wants me back.

Here Goes Nothing

Tonight, I went with Gary to the Rock and saw the old man; he said, "I haven't seen you around; what's going on." I heard your looking (before I finished, he turned to me and said), Are you interested?

I will be available in 2 weeks, and the old man replied, "Lucky it's the summer I can hold back, don't say nothing to that jerk off in the booth; I'll tell him." I guess he did miss me.

I did It

I made the call to the station today and gave in my notice, and my boss said, "I hope you're not leaving because of the incidents." I told him no overnights are just getting to me.

I stopped by Singer's and told him I gave my notice today, and he replied, "I got the call this morning to see if I got anyone." "Damn, that was quick," I replied.

I saw Pork Chops in the studio, and when he came out and I said WH is looking, and he turned to and said, "I got an interview tomorrow." I was glad for him, and I warned him about the morning guy what a heartless business we live in.

ROUND

TWO

Déjà Vu

What a fucking night; nothing ever changes at that place. My first night was almost my last night. Thank god Gary was there, or I would of probably would have got killed.

Things were going good; the regulars were coming over and said they were glad we were back and there were delighted CD boy was gone.

WTF, I ask Gary, "Is that ice coming in here?" and then I noticed two drunken assholes laughing and throw ice cubes at the booth. Now, you don't have to be a DJ to know water and electricity don't mix; there goes your equipment. I yell over to them, "HEY JERK OFFS, KNOCK IT OFF."

Then I see the old man looking at me and then came to the booth. I told him what they are doing, and he told me to calm down; WTF. I responded, "If my shit goes down, you ain't going to replace it; you'll complain I have cheap equipment.

Things settle for a minute, and I was telling Gary, "If these..." before I finished, I was out of the booth and jacking this clown up against the wall and telling him, "If you throw and MUTHER FUCKING ICE CUBE, I WILL PLANT IT UP YOUR ASS AND MAKE YOUR MOUTH AS THE DESPINSOR."

Before I knew it, Gary take me off the asshole, and the old man said to settle the fuck down; I told him, "You fucking want me back, and tonight could be the last if you don't hand your business." The old man finally threw them out, and the bar applauded, and drinks were flowing to the DJ booth; the chant of "HE'S BACK" echoed through the bar, and the old man looked like what I did in bringing him back.

I wasn't the same guy as before, and I had an edge on me knowing I am right, and I am not taking the shit from whomever. I looked around the booth and noticed a CD; I asked the bar what I should do with this thing, "Break It, Break It," I smacked it against my corner, and nothing; I tried again. It bent; I said, "WTF, he's gone anyway, and the head jerk off is back," I dumped it over the booth, and people were coming up and stomping on it.

Dam that felt good. I haven't done that in a long time. Later during the night, I told Gary I got a call from my booty call chick; she wants to meet later. We survived the night and needed to unwind, so we drove to see the overnight jock to the radio station. When we got to the station, Gary prompted me to call her, and when I did, I explained my buddy is in town, and we are celebrating his birthday; she replied, "Bring him along."

You Want to Do What?

The old man approached me and wanted to start an oldies night on Tuesdays, beginning in September. I hate fucking oldies; you're lucky to get a song longer than two and a half minutes.

It's Tuesday Night Oldies

The sort of good thing that happened was she came in tonight, and I said it had been a long time, and she was telling him she was trying to get her shit together, and I was right about telling her in focusing on her son.

I felt like I was on speed because of these songs' length, but the crowd we had enjoyed it, and the old man was happy.

I Got A Bright Idea

I went to Singers to see if Pork Chops was in tonight, and as I walked in, I heard that voice over the house speakers; when he finished his session, he came out of the studio, I ask him, "If he wants to pick up a night at the Rock, doing oldies."

Singer told him, "Don't do it." I said, "If your free next week and hang with me, and I'll have you throw some on and see if you like it." We agreed, and I know the old man would have to hear someone before letting another step in. He asks me, why don't I don't want to do it?" "Simple, oldies is not my thing, and two months of this shit was enough," I replied.

See What Happens

Here comes Pork Chops strolling into the bar like a lamb going into the wolf pack.

I introduced him to Jr., and once he got settled in, I said, show me what you got.

He looked at me and said, "You know I'm not like you, shit, brother, you're saying things. I would need a bodyguard to protect me."

PC was smooth on the mic and had a nice flow. He was mixing it up with the crowd but not matching my style. I was joking with him, saying, "Were like Donny and Marie, You're a little sugar, and I'm all hardcore." The funny thing was it worked, and he was the jock I always wanted to be, have the words flow like silk.

I went over to Jr. and said, what do you think, "My father won't have a problem, and he'll probably want to squeeze you out another night." Some would be a threat, but I took it as a compliment to have quality jocks working for me.

Am I Seeing What I'm Seeing????

I came into the bar, and the old man said, "I heard you hired your replacement; my kid likes him." I just looked at him and said, "Remember, there's only one Domino (and walked into my booth)." I liked having someone in-house that can keep me sharp and step up my game.

I felt like I had to prove myself, and once I started, I had the crowd doing what I wanted, and suddenly, I noticed something weird. I was playing "Bon Jovi" and saw this chick straddling her man. At times her head was buried into his back right in front of the booth. Now being a people observer, I continued to watch, "No Shit, she's banging this Dude," I said to myself. I decided to have some fun. I had a sex sound effects cd and started to play moans underneath the Bon Jovi. Tommy (the bartender) looked at me, and I slightly nodded in the direction of the lovebirds. He started to laugh and told the old man.

The old man (the only way he could approach the couple) said, "Can you take it to the parking lot, or I will have a line starting behind you."

The funny thing was that most of the bar didn't know what the hell was going on, and the old man called them pigs for something he does in his bar.

No Shit Look Who It Is?

A typical Thursday night, and I looked across the bar and saw her. I singled over to Tommy to give her a drink on me. She did stop by and told me she was getting her shit together and was in nurse's school, thanks to me. She told me I helped her wake up about my responsibilities.

I was happy for her. She did say she won't be a stranger and we have to get together when she's free and have some fun.

Let's See Pork Chops

I went out with Bones and the boys, and we ended up at the Rock to bust on Pork Chops.

He had a friendly crowd for a Tuesday, and I was just glad it wasn't me playing this shit. I always enjoy a person that can entertain, and PC can; I think his style complements mine and vice versa because we are so different. The boys were busting my balls, saying, "Are you taking notes." I replied, "No, I just thinking if you came over here and got on your knees, no one would think any different with that flowing hair of yours." Flynn just looked like me and smiled. I was thinking, did I waste a good line.

What Happened?

Tonight, I saw those girls telling me about the DJ awards a while ago, and I walked over and asked what happened with that. The one girl told me, "Good news, bad news, you would have won 3 out of four categories, and when Tony found out, he squashed the whole event," she asks, "What did you do to him." I just replied, "I didn't want to be one of his bitches (and I walked away)."

It sucks in this business the jealousy level has to be so high; when I walk into another bar, I go to hang and see what I can care about taking the DJ's job. But, some jocks, when they notice you, they get all insecure and shit. I use that energy to fuel my fire, and I always step up my game to another level when the prima donnas' come to my house.

Looking at my little team, I put together everybody who has their unique part in the cog. Some are not mic gifted, but they know their music and know how to hold a crowd. Things are pretty good the second time around, and I can work at the station and take off a night here and there.

No Way You're Asking Me, What?

It's a typical Wednesday night; the crowd is rocking and gets approached by this blonde tonight, but it wasn't the usual proposal; she wanted to off me a job at another bar. This shocked the shit out of me, I knew I had the talent, but the old man kept me grounded by saying, "This is the only place that wants you."

I have to think about it, and she said, "Come by one night and talk to the owner, and by the way, we told him all about you, and he sent us over to talk to you."

Time To Regroup And Plan

I got a call from Hot Traxx and told him about my circumstance and suggested doing what feels right. He also invited me over to his compound to see his studio. We made a date in a couple of cassettes; maybe that's what I needed a diversion; speaking of diversions, I needed to call Gary.

I told Gary about the situation and said if it works, I need you to do a night at the Rock, and I would do the other; right now, all they want is Friday and Saturday nights.

Gary asked, "What about the old man." "Fuck him, at this point for nearly three years, all I have been hearing from him is that he made me, and I'm nobody without him; I think it's time to let him eat his own words." Gary looked at me and said, "When are we going."

The Meet

My philosophy in life is if someone wants to talk, well, then I'll listen. I went over with Gary to meet Jimmy (the Sportsman's Bar owner); the talk was quick; the only thing I ask was to give me a week to tell the old man and get my shit in order, also the only way I know he will let me do one night elsewhere if he can choose.

I walked out and was impressed with the bar, but it didn't have a DJ booth, but I was promised if I'm as good as they say, Jimmy will build me one. I told Gary we have PC on Tuesday,

Wednesday, and Thursday is my night. I prefer to do Friday at the Rock, and You do Saturday night at Sportsman's; the only thing is the old man could tell me go fuck myself and throw me out, but at least I already have a place to go. We also have a couple of backup jocks now on payroll, so I am at the right place.

The Talk with The Old Man

I sat down with the old man before I'd started tonight and discussed the situation.

He acted like it didn't bother him, but I can tell he was pissed, like a dejected ex-girlfriend. I told him, "I would like him to choose the night he wanted me there." He said, "I would prefer PC, then Gary," but I explained PC is only available on Tuesday nights right now, but if it changes, I will notify the schedule.

I also told him booth bars are different in music. Sportsman is more poppy and classic Rock, and you guys have more of an edge in the music.

Road Trip

I went to the Hot Traxx house tonight to get away from the bar business and have some real fun. I was jealous of Hot Traxx because he was a mixer, something I could never do, but he was reluctant to teach me, and I felt comfortable to look a fool in front of him.

My mixes were like a 50-car pileup on the turnpike with the jungle drums playing. We had in common our ears for music; we would break songs before they hit the radio.

Hot Traxx was doing mix shows for three radio stations, and I tossed a lot of stuff back and forth while doing the bar scene. He would tell me he would never think about using certain songs in the mix before.

A New

CHAPTER

BEGINS

WHY And Why Wouldn't It?

It was my first night at the Sportsman's, and of course, nothing could go smoothly for me. First, we are experiencing a massive snowstorm. My cousin was helping me transport the equipment to the new bar, and of course, I had to go to the Rock to get some stuff, and the old man kept telling me, "You better not take any of the good stuff out of here." I replied, "Unless we turned into the Granada overnight."

Thank god the bars weren't that far from each other I saw Jimmy when we got there and ask him if he was still going to be open; he replied, "We are a neighborhood bar, and they will walk here, especially being stuck in their houses all day."

Now here's when the fun started, my cousin's car started to go sideways down the street, and he said, "What do you want from a mustang in the snow. I said, "That didn't do that before. He replied, "Remember, we had a car full of records and equipment."

I finally got home thought I was going to relax before I had to go in. The phone kept ringing; stupid me, all my DJ's work for either the township or the county, and they are on snow removal until tomorrow. WTF, it's me myself and I, but wait a minute, I called PC and begged him, lucky he was free, and now he had to drive in 45 minutes in the remains of a blizzard.

The funny thing about PC is that he did not know the metal or the majority of the new music unless played in a Go-Go bar.

I told him I would go to the Rock and put cue cards on the hot records and tell you what to play and not. If you don't know it or are unsure, say I have it. I told him the old man is working and doesn't like the crazy mental, so cue it before playing it.

I finally made it to the Sportsman's and settled in meeting the new victims (bartenders). The only thing that sucked was the setup. I was in another room far away from the action and wondered how this would work.

The night started slow, and before I knew it, the bar was packed, and the backroom started getting the overflow. I was in my groove and was light on my verbal attacks unless I knew my target. I met this guy hanging near my booth set up for most of the night; he was shooting pool and filling me in on some crowd.

Here we go; a couple of guys approached me and said they used to DJ and their good friends with Jimmy and commented the crowd is usually not this crowded. My interpretation was because they sucked, and Jimmy decided to move on.

I survived my first night, and Jimmy was pleased; he said, "The bar hit a record for its nightly take, and the girls were pleased they made a boatload on tips. Let's see what you can do without a snowstorm."

Why can't I ever get a good job? Are these owners all the same?

The Next Day

I woke up this morning feeling reborn—all the doubts of my being erased.

I was the best and knew how to move a crowd, whether for the first time or nights over. I didn't feel my ego was enormous, but my confidence was shining.

All these years, the old man told me I was nothing without him; where the fuck was he last night. I walked into a room with limited information and lit it up.

I walked in the Rock and stopped to talk to the old man to see how things went last night. He said, "Why did you take all the good records with you."

You mean the shit you don't like, plus PC doesn't know that shit, so I put cue cards on the albums which songs were good and which ones to stay away from; plus I told him to play the singles instead of the albums and blame it on me." Then, I walked him to the booth to show him; I knew he would be like that.

The bar was packed, and I thought it was time for payback to the old man.

I grabbed the mic, "I heard the old man was upset last night because he couldn't hear one of his favorite songs, and I'm not talking about Sinatra.

Here you go, pops, I dropped the needle, and on came Metallica and Master of Puppets (the mental heads went nuts because they knew he hated that song)" I guess I am the puppet master because he gave me a look get this shit off, but plastered that fake smile to the metalheads. After I finished, I ran out and went to the Sportsman's to see how Gary made out. Jimmy said, "He's not you, but he did okay." WTF, here we go again; Gary is not strong on the mic; he would make announcements, but that's it. Me, I can cut a 300 person crowd to silence with few words. I know not everyone has a gift to entertain, and for me, it was always there, but it took a couple of years to perfect this game.

I Thought Nobody Can Top Those Guys

I'd worked at the Rock for close to 4 years, and though the bar was full of characters that could not be topped, boy was I wrong. In the recent week, I got to know Wojo, Bobby, the Hot Dog Man (aka fan man), Jimmy, and the ladies behind the bar, otherwise known as the bar wrenches.

Tonight, after hours, I got to see the fan man in action. Wojo said to me, look at that fan. Do you notice anything wrong with it? I looked up, and it was all bent. Wojo yelled, "Come on, Fan, man, it's time for a ride." Wojo picked Bobby up, and suddenly, he started going around the fan, but nobody was pushing him; it was all under the fan's power. Now, Bobby was close to 5 feet tall and 95 pounds if he was soaking wet.

After I finished, I ran out and went to the Sportsman's to see how Gary made out. Jimmy said, "He's not you, but he did okay." WTF, here we go again; Gary is not strong on the mic; he would make announcements, but that's it. Me, I can cut a 300-person crowd to silence with few words. I know not everyone has a gift to entertain, and for me, it was always there, but it took a couple of years to perfect this game.

Another Record Night

Jimmy came over and said, "I've never seen it like this before; every Friday night, you break last week's record, only if we can pick it up on Saturdays." I wonder what is wrong, and he told me the numbers are good, and the crowd is steady, but Gary doesn't put the show on to stimulate drinks. I told him, "I will talk to Gary about stepping up his game."

Now What?

It's been two months now, and I thought everything was going well at both bars until I walked in the Rock tonight. The old man told me to get rid of Gary, "He's not working out. It seems he's more interested in picking up these sluts than playing music." He also inquired about why PC can't do it.

I told him he works those nights unless something breaks; he's not available.

I can see if Bones or Lou can do it.

He agreed if he got Gary out quickly. Now I have to tell Gary no more Friday nights.

Here We Go To Singers'

    I went over to Singers to see if he had anybody to jock on Fridays at the Rock, I saw Jeff, and I knew him from years ago. I told him what I needed and wanted to give it a shot. I told him to show up next Friday, and I was impressed he did know his music.

Audition Night

I met Jeff over at the Rock and introduced him to the old man; I hung out for a while until he got settled in and told the old man I'll be back in an hour, let the kid have some breathing room.

When I came back, the old man grabbed me and said, "Get that fucking kid out of her because if I hear Good Evening one more time, I'll go over and introduce Count Dracula with microphone permanently shoved down his goddam throat."

"So, I guess you didn't like him," I inquired as I walked to the booth. I told Jeff, good job, and I'll take over; I'll call you in a couple of days and tell him what the old man said.

Me being the ball buster that I am, as soon as the kid left, I took the mic and said, "Good Evening, I'm DOMINNNNNNNO." All

I saw was the old man giving me the finger, and I replied, "Mikeeee, he likes me."

Temporary Fix

I got Lou to fill in for a couple of weeks because he lived over an hour away and could not do this permanently, but the old man was happy when I told him. Now, I can concentrate on getting Gary up to speed, yeah, right.

Jimmy approached me tonight and pulled me into the kitchen. He reminded me of over conversation and said it's time to make a change. NOOOOOOOOOOOOOOOOOOOOO.

After shuffling the cards at the Rock, now Jimmy wants me only for Friday and Saturday nights.

The Day Is Saved Thanks to Pork Chops

I made that dreadful phone call to PC, and it was surprisingly pleasant. He told me his availability has just opened up and was available more nights. I offered him Thursday and Saturday nights at the Rock.

When I came into the Rock, I spoke to the old man and told him. I have PC on Thursday and Saturday nights; he looked at me strangely. "I thought Thursday nights were your nights?"

Jimmy wants me to do Friday and Saturday nights, and I thought this was a good compromise since you like PC; I got him for two power nights."

I also convinced the old man Tuesdays were consistent with the bowlers, and the league would be over in two weeks, and I can have Bones do Tuesdays.

He asked, "Who's doing Fridays?" I responded with one word, "Lou." He was a little concerned about having Bones work a night but said he would give it a shot. Goddam, I'm okay doing the DJ shuffle. Now I got to tell Gary for the second time in 2 weeks he's fired, but now he can do his favorite thing pick up girls and drink.

Can I Breathe

I think the drama is over for now or until someone screws up. The only shit I hear about every Wednesday night when I'm working at the Rock, "Is why do you take all the good records for the other place," by the old man. This is coming from a grown-ass man, talking like he was the scorned ex.

I had to shut this down for one last time. I ask, "Did Bones tell you for the past two months every Monday we have been going record shopping and he has been picking the records for here, and the other guys I would give them 20 bucks to pick out what they wanted, so WHAT THE FUCK ARE YOU TALKING ABOUT?????"

At the highpoint of the night, she came in and was surprised I was still here.

I told her only on Wednesday nights. So, I ask, "When are we going to hang?" She replied, "Mondays are the best night." I suggested I get out of town, and I owe Lou a dinner, so if you're up to around two with Lou, he'll be with his girlfriend this time. I can't believe she said yes, and she was looking better than ever.

Hibachi and The Track

I told Lou to pick the restaurant, boy. Was that a mistake? I wanted to be nice and repay a favor since he helped me for two months at the bar.

Lou's favorite restaurant was TGIF, so I told her she wouldn't be surprised if we ended up there; boy, the joke was on me.

We get to Lou's, and he asks if we have ever been to a hibachi restaurant, and we said no, but was up for a good time.

Now, Lou can be on the cheap side but spare no expense when someone treats him. We made it to the joint and had a great time until the check came. I was prepared for a 60 to 80 dollar tab, not a buck fifty.

I turned to her and said, "WTF? He set me up." I had the money but wasn't going to be taken advantage of, so I threw a buck 20 on the table and said, "Can cover the rest." Big spender had to ask his girl for money because he expected me to cover it all. "I told him you should have told me it was going to be pricier than your usual hang out. I had more money but fucked him for taking advantage. The funny thing he suggested was to go to the racetrack after dinner, but he asks if we can stop by the bank because he didn't think he needed money for dinner.

The night turned out nice; we missed the trifecta by a nose. After dropping off moneybags, I offered to stop by the Sportsman for a nightcap on the way home. I told her to pick the horses, and I will pay; we almost won 15 hundred. She asks, "If the Rock wasn't good for me anymore."

It was a good time and the same result. Dummy went home with blue balls.

I Got the Hook Up

This week, I got a good score, and I even cut a deal for the Rock to be in with it. I went into the Rock and, of course, got greeted by the old man, "Why can't you give us any movie tickets for giveaways." I replied, "Whatever jerk off told you don't know shit, I was going to offer you some tickets tonight to use for Wednesdays and Saturday night, and I was going to let you pick what movies you want; shit, your worst than an ex-girlfriend." He said, "Thanks, of course, you would keep some for the night."

"You pick the fucking nights, I don't give a shit, try to be a nice guy," and I walked away.

You Said If I Bring Them You Will Build It

After a fruitful night at the Sportsman, I grabbed Jimmy and said, "Hey Ronald McDonald, when are you going to build my playhouse (that was my nickname for Jimmy; he had a red afro). He responded, "You're lucky you're making me some. I think it's time to move you to the front of the house."

I saw my stalker again, we have become good friends and were hanging out, plus I felt like I had a bodyguard when he was around; Randy stood 6 foot 7 and weighed close to 300 pounds.

Everyone Still Hung Over

Last night was crazy. The Sportsman after hours was worse than regular hours with the customers. Jimmy would have a select crew hang after, and we would play the games in the back room for free. Wojo passed out before I left, and I didn't get out of there by 4:30 in the morning and returned around 10:30 to do my record inventory; when I got in, Wojo looked like shit (he was the day bartender, and he would cook sometimes), he asks can you make burgers and steaks for the lunch crowd. I figured what the hell? I'll take one for the team.

The lunch crowd started to come in, and people were busting chops, "Where the hell is my burger." I walked out of the kitchen and said, "If you want to hear your shit tonight, Shut the hell up and have another beer." I walked back into the kitchen, and I heard someone yell, "I guess that's what happens when you play shitty songs." I yelled back, "But I don't have to eat it,"

Jimmy came in and said, "What the hell are you doing? These steaks cost money; stop doubling the order." I looked at Jimmy and said, "I'm Italian with a heavy hand."

His wife asks me if I can make a Rubin; I said a "what" and then told me how to do it. Later that night, Jimmy would yell out, "Hey BJ, at least you have a second career; go make me a pizza."

I was having fun at a bar and didn't feel like it was a drain to get up every night to "perform."

The Day Finally Came

I went to the Sportsman's early this morning and met with the crew building my DJ booth. "Are you fucking serious? It was two of the regulars, and they were a couple lucky for me; she wasn't as drunk as her boyfriend was. I was nervous the whole time, and they weren't listening to how this was supposed to have a barrier wall to take the vibration and bumps.

It was around five, and I had about 4 hours to go home and relax; Jimmy told me, "Hey BJ, I expect you to use it tonight." Now I had to rewire the speakers, hook up the equipment, do a soundcheck, and put the records in some order tonight that works.

After all the aggravation, it felt like home, besides having the records skipping as a heavy foot walked by or if someone leaned into the booth. I thought I was in action, and I can control the crowd better. Now Domino can come out and play.

Oldie But A Goodie

I was big-time and always had an opening act and decided to play the jukebox game at the Sportsman. I had someone; usually, the bouncer, stand next to the plug, and when I gave my signal, he would unplug, and I would play a song to match the volume, and every song brings up the volume until they realized I was playing. Some night I would say cut that beast; it's time for armature hour.

Jimmy would laugh because some people would still go to the jukebox and then complain, "why their songs aren't being played?" I told Jimmy that I did an old game at the Rock, and people would get pissed. "Hey, stupid when the lights are off, doesn't that mean; it's turned off, DUDDDH."

Who's That Girl?

I like being upfront. You can see all the lovelies and connect with them, not like I have the courage to make a move. I noticed I knew some of the crowd she was hanging with, and that would make it easy for me to say hi. It was déjà vu all over again because it only took me 10 minutes before I approached her.

I knew 2 out of the three girls, and they introduced me to the stranger as Miss New Jersey (she didn't look like a typical pageant contestant; she was thick but very pleasing).

I got back into the booth, and guess who comes walking in the door? Yes, her.

I put on one of her favorites from "The Babies,' and she looked up with a big smile (maybe tonight is the night.)

Ben (the bouncer) came up to me and said, "Who the fuck is that girl? It doesn't matter because, by the end of the night, she's mine." I laughed to myself; I thought I heard this song before.

She came up to the booth and asked if I can take her home because she didn't want to go to the Rock. I sent her a couple of Dr. Peppers (the house specialty), but she made me have one with her.

I'm now thinking, could this be the night. I ended the night, and by what means I don't know how, Ben made it in my car. She kept busting my balls and telling me my mother can't' help me tonight because the sharks are swimming.

We got back to her place, and she was flirtier with Ben, and I still thought he would get some, but she had other plans. She tried to go upstairs but didn't make it; her sister caught her and said it's time to go, and then I heard her throwing up another typical night with her again. We get in the car, and Ben goes to me, "I would have still done here; let's go get some breakfast.

He Does What?

    I worked on the beer truck with my father today, and one the driver approached me and was asking all kinds of questions about Ben the bouncer, he told me, "If you see him, you call me he owes me 500 bucks, and I'm getting it one way or another." By the way, this guy is a local bookie; my father said to turn him over because that was your warning if you are around.

Up, Up And Oh, Snap....My Balls

Tonight was crazy. Jimmy and his boys, after he closed the kitchen, were party hard. I knew I would be in trouble because he wanted to hear Bruce or Billy Joel when he was drunk, so I would play them to keep him quiet, the bad thing was the group would sound like a karaoke nightmare, but the bar enjoyed the show.

The fan man came up and was plastered and spat out the request of, "When are you going to play some shit? We all known." I just turned my back and continued. I was battering the bartenders tonight with the "Bar Wrench" title (it was a plaque Jimmy had at the front of the bar, and that's what we referred to the bartenders as). One of them was giving me hard looks like it was agitating her.

At the end of the night, I saw Fan Man walking around with a long, brass foot pole from the pole. He said, "See my pole....do you see my pole. Get the fuck back cause I'm going to jump over the bar with my pole." Before you knew it, the crowd parted, and Fan Man ran from the backroom looking Bruce Jenner in the Olympics, and when he approached the bar, he made a foot in the air, and the door was planted in his crotch, you just heard all the males in the room say, "Ohhh Fuck."

After hours I was talking to the bartenders and ask what's going on. The one said, "She was in a bad mood, and that wasn't helping, and besides the fact you're nothing more than a male socialist pig that makes us money, so I take it." That hit me because what I did was for fun and nobody's expense.

I told her, you should know me by now when I'm on the mic. It's him, and now it's me. The other girls told me I was okay. She gets like this cause of her boyfriend's prissy mood; Jimmy doesn't even want him in the bar when she is working.

The Presidents Men Are Coming

Gary called me earlier to warn me; his brother was home with 6 of his brothers in arms (they were presidential security from the marines); when they come out, all they want to do is party and look for some fun.

I told Jimmy, "All the DJ's Men" were coming in tonight, and he remembers the last time they were in. He told me to have them come to the bar, and he would put them on the ABC list as bouncers so that they won't get in any trouble.

I always felt safe when they were in because, frankly, if they were good for the President, they were good for me.

The boys came in, and Jimmy told them the plan and said the drinks are on the house. They were hanging in the bleachers next to the booth. I got this jerk off wanting Led Zeppelin, but the groove wasn't right at the time. So 20 minutes later, he came up and said, "Where the FUCK is my song," I replied, "With that attitude, you can GO FUCK YOURSELF." I turned around to the records, and suddenly, you hear this loud BANG and a voice saying, "If you move, you will die."

I looked over the DJ booth, and it was that jerk off with the President's Men holding a vital spot; they picked him up, and Jimmy signaled to get rid of him; they turned the corner, and you hear another loud bang followed by, "I thought you were going to open the door."

Jimmy yelled to the bartenders, "To take care of my DJ's men."

What I found out was he was getting ready to throw his beer bottle at me, and the boys swooped in and took him down. It was funny the rest of the night; nobody was coming up to ask for a request until they heard what happened.

Am I That Bad?

I got taken back from the comments from one of the bartenders the other night. I always took on another persona when that microphone was on. I wouldn't say I like socialist pigs; I believe in equal rights, opening up that door, and treating any woman like the princess they are, except when he comes out. I don't understand where I can call someone out for doing dirty deeds under the bar, and then she comes over ready to yell at me, and I pointed to her chair and said, there something waiting for you. Now, that's messed up; I just got done saying, "Hey is there a line over there? If not, I'm next."

Where can you make good coin and call people every name in the book and buy them a drink, and all is good? Are people that starve for attention? I wonder how I make it to my car safe at times.

I did talk to the bartender, and she was alright; she said her man gets pissed and gives her shit after. I said he should come to me; I would respect that.

My House Is More Dangerous Than The Bar

I got home around 3:30 this morning, and when I was walking up the stairs, I heard my name being called, and I acknowledged it. "Get the fuck in here," my uncle bellowed.

As I walked into his bedroom, I saw a gun pointed at me. My uncle told me, "You were quiet walking up the stairs, and I didn't think it was you; the next fucking time, do not be so soft because I don't want to explain to your father I shot you." As they say in an Italian family, don't ask and don't tell.

It's Me

I'm not taking any chances tonight; when I was walking up the stairs, I was knocking on the walls and calling out Sneak, hey Sneak (that was my uncle's nickname), I heard that voice again telling me to get over here.

"Now that was much better, see no drama," my uncle told me. I ask, "I wonder if I woke up, aunt Mary; his response was, "fuck her, I'm worried about my ass."

It's 2:00 a.m.; what Do You Want?

Tonight, I was ready to kill Jimmy; I told him if this girl calls (the new bouncer's ex-girlfriend, but he stills bangs her), I'm not here. I'm sitting at the bar enjoying my Dr. Pepper, and of course, the phone rings; Jimmy answers, and all I hear is, "Yes, he's right here." I got on the phone, and she wanted me to come over to her house, she also added that her kid and mother would be home, but they want to bother us as long as we keep the noise done.

I told her I am going home now because I got to get up early tomorrow, maybe a rain check. She said, really, "You're going to miss the blowjob of your life....click."

Do You Want To Move In

Lou called me today and asked if I wanted to move in because his roommate is moving out in a month. I decided to say yes without thinking because he lived at least an hour away, and I would have to make that drive every night.

He said it would be nice to paint it before moving in, and I figured I could get Randy to go for extra help. I asked him tonight, and he said no problem but has to be on a Monday and Tuesday, but of us worked in the bar business, but he was a bouncer in a gentleman's club (Studio 27).

The Phone Will Find You

I talked to Randy, and we went up tonight to paint the apartment, and someone called Randy to tell him about Miss NJ's house burned down. I felt terrible because she lost every, including all of her pageant wear. I said their good people; let me call Jimmy and see if he wanted to do a fundraiser at the bar; I told him it would be a good pub.

The only problem was the pageant was in 2 two weeks, and we only had five days to pool this off. What does a great planner do? We played "OH, Shit, Fuck," while watching porn to discuss strategies. By the way, the game is simple; anytime you hear those magical words, you take a shot. Besides the porn, beer, and painting, Our new mission is to save Miss New Jersey.

I Can't Believe It

I went over a last-minute adjustment with Jimmy and Randy. Jimmy told me her girlfriends want to do something.

I told him we were covered, but if they wish to go ahead, they wanted to get lunch meat and sell sandwiches; I looked at Jimmy and said, your stuff isn't good enough. Jimmy was already in with discounted drinks and giving total tilt for an hour to the cause.

I told him you wanted a circus; I got every local TV and radio station to come here. Randy has his girls from Studio 27 (the dancers) to meet and mingle; we will sell pictures for five bucks. Many local businesses donate prizes for door prizes and the higher value, and we will auction them off. I also have some local bands coming out not to play but hang out. Plus, I have a couple of my bitter DJs coming down to help me out. Jimmy looked at me and said, "You did this in less than five days."

The Big Top Is In

I'm glad that is over, tonight was the big fundraiser, and it was off the hook; NBC, ABC, CBS, Channel 11, and WPST (local radio station) all showed up.

I went in earlier to finish setting up, and some reporters were there looking for pre-interviews; one lady was getting all the action and acting like this was her show, taking all the credit for tonight's event. I ask Randy, "Who the hell is this woman?" later to find out it was Miss NJ's boss. A reported walked by Randy, and I overheard him ask, "Do you want to meet the man that put this whole thing together? the response was funny (after he took a long look at me). "No, I just did." I told Randy, "it's time to go home and get dolled up so they will take us seriously."

We came back to the bar, and people were lining up outside, and Jimmy told me, "Good job, I wanted a circus, and I got one." The night moves quickly without any snags, except for twisted tongue; I got emotional at times and wasn't my smoothest. Miss NJ, I didn't have any contact with her, and the big hit was the Studio 52 girls; I got five packs of 10 instant films, and we sold out quick for $5.00 bucks. The guys didn't complain. Overall we raised over 5 thousand dollars, and she also got all of her wardrobes. We were so packed and didn't know until the end of the night we had a line around the corner, and people were waiting for a couple of hours to get in, and I heard Randy and the girls went out to entertain the outside crowd. It was a blast.

The After Math

I got up early and went over to the Sportsman to hear the final damage. Jimmy was in the kitchen and gave me the 411. He said, "Your Miss NJ came in to ask for her MONEY, took it and left, did not say one word in how she was glad or appreciated in us helping her out, she did tell me she is going to the shore and will be back in a couple of days."

WTF, did we pay for the bitch's shore trip? Anyway, Jimmy was pleased, and so was I, in how long it took and how well it was.

Do You Want To Go?

Miss NJ came into the bar and was nice to me; she invited Randy and me to go to the Miss New Jersey pageant next weekend. I had to ask Jimmy for the weekend off, and he said if Lou can fill in and, of course, you can for the work you did for that bitch.

Randy came into the bar later, and I ask if he had any plans for next week because we just got invited to go to the beauty pageant.

We Survived

We stopped at the Sportsman's from our long weekend at the New Jersey Pageant; Jimmy asked how it goes; it was cool and filled with drunkenness.

Our theme was, "You can take the boys out of Trenton, but you can take Trenton out of the boys." I showed Jimmy the picture of our bathroom sink filled with beer; he said, "That's how I roll."

Jimmy asks, "Did my BJ get laid?" Randy told him, no, and I told her girlfriend if my man doesn't get anything, he wasn't giving her anything." We found out that the pig was getting trained in another room by some strangers she picked up on.

I told him it was a good time my sister station was doing the oldies show at the hotel bar, and we were treated like V,I,P.'s I also added these women were crazy behind the stage, we were standing there, and they were adjusting their boobs and g strings like we were never there. Randy was ready to ask if he could help this smoking Puerto Rican, but I bet she would think of beat the shit out of him or drop to her knees if her padre wasn't there.

I Got an Offer

My mom called me today and said with her and Guy getting married, he wanted to see if you wanted to rent the condo. I thought that was good but needed to get a roommate.

I talked to Randy when we were at Lou's, and he wanted to move out of his house, so I called him today, and he agreed. Now I got to tell Lou I changed my mind; he still has a month to find another roommate.

I called Lou and told him the news, and he was pissed, and I told him I could give him two months' rent to cover until he finds a roommate and throw him some days at the Sportsman to help him financially. I thought that was fair because I was an idiot to agree with this in the first place.

Almost A Year

What a year this has been, I started out having three other jocks with me, and one bar, now 12 jocks and 2 bars, and I'm managing one and playing at the other exclusively. I was proud of myself for who and where I started but not completely satisfied because I could have extended in doing more mobile parties but did not have the right people to fit that niche.

The old man wasn't happy. I took myself out of his place, but I couldn't take his abuse and kept the Rock because of the status. I think the old man got mad when I fired his cousin because that jackass acted like a two-year-old and scratch all of the new records we bought because he wasn't invited to go, but we dropped off the records back to the bar so he could be the first to use them. When I heard all the records were destroyed and bragged to Bones, he did it; I told the old man he was gone. The old man looked at me and said over some shitty records. I replied, "Good, then you can give me 200 bucks to replace them shitty records I bought for your joint."

Of course, he just laughed and walked away, and I did what I needed to do.

Is This The Rock Or Sportsman's

It was a typical Saturday night at the Sportsman's until these drunk get their panties in a twist. I saw that John (the bouncer) was having an issue with two guys; I signaled to another bouncer and couldn't get his attention; I got out of the booth, saw Jimmy, and pointed to the far corner, lucky I got there, John had one kid. The other was ready to clock him in the back of the head. I hooked his arm and took him down to the ground.

Before I knew it, we were at the door behind a crowd like me. The other two bouncers were peeling people off of the pile; Holy Shit, I felt this pull of energy coming from the door and found myself on the bottom of the bank with Chubs (a bouncer that was 6 foot 2 over 300 pounds) sitting on my face with my hands cupped like a chair. I yelled up to him, and with whatever strength I had left, throw him onto the sidewalk.

I got up felt like my head was used as a basketball on the concrete. I asked, "Who the fuck opened the door???!!??" When you tossed the guy, John walked over and said I ran around to the back exit and then figured I could help by opening the front door.

"Hey, dummy, by doing that, we all were pulled forward," I explained to him. Jimmy looked at me and said, "What happened to my BJ? You better stick to records. I can't afford to have you out." Later, I thought to myself I should have dogged his girl, only if I knew.

Hey Goombah, What's Your Problem?

I asked Jimmy tonight, did you see what the two bone crunchers did to me. He said I heard a loud noise coming out of the kitchen.

I told him the one dirtbag tossed a beer bottle at them both, and he asked do you know them? And he continued to say they are low grade; you don't want to fuck with them because they could be collecting their bones. He pulled me into the office and said, tonight, my lady and I would be walking you out to your car. I said, "That's nice, but who's going to watch my back driving home."

I saw my uncle was still up when I got home, told him what happened, and described what the two Guido's looked like. My uncle said, "Done, but if you have an issue again, tell me, and it will be over." I felt like I just confessed to the godfather.

Another Offer Comes My Way

I went into the radio station today and worked in production, Jack (the program director) told me the station would start changing the format, and the morning show would be all talk. They needed someone to ride the board and wanted to see if I was interested. I was a little surprised because I rarely worked on any live shows in that studio but was excited about the opportunity.

I had a couple of days to think about it, and the person I was going to work with was known as the voice of central jersey. Currently, he was working in Florida and coming back to the station for the show. I think I was more nervous about working with him, but the opportunity was to learn from the best. I was also told that there would be a producer, Ruth Ann Williams (her husband was Bruce Williams, an immense national talent and started at CTC in his early years), so all I had to do is run the show's technique portion.

I Need To Set The Rules

It's been a couple of weeks that Randy and I moved in, and I told him I don't care who he brings back from the club, but Thursday Nights are off-limits because I work Sportsman and then have 2 hours to take a nap and do the morning show. He agreed, and tonight he broke the rules.

It's around 2:30 and finally got to sleep, and then I heard, but worry, my roommate is sleeping, he won't wake up.

This asshole will do this bitch in front of me, and all I want to do is sleep. Since I couldn't sleep now, let's have some fun. I heard a loud banging noise and got up like the undertaker to see what the hell is going on. I listened to this soft voice say, "I think your roommate is up," Randy replied, "He does that in his sleep; he also talks in his sleep at times."

All I saw was Randy ramming her head into the wall and then telling her I want to give you pleasure, not pain." At this point, I took the pillow over my mouth and laughed wear it sounded like a loud fart.

This chick had no clue I kept looking at the clock, and it was getting closer to 4 am; lucky, he finally stopped around 3:30 to give me a 30-minute nap.

I left, and I decided to look at this creature that kept me up all night. I went and gave props to Randy for his conquest. I came into the studio, and Jack said, "You look like shit, didn't you sleep?" I told him about my tails, and he said to be young again, then he said, "Tell your roommate to knock this shit off because I need you wide awake. When I got home, I told Randy I couldn't do this anymore because I only have maybe 3 hours to get a quick nap and then go into the station on Thursday nights. If you need to bring in your strays, you got the living room, but no more in the bedroom and also, Sunday nights low key when I go to be at 8 pm, Jesus I sound like an old man, to bed by 8 pm at the age of 25.

I Got An Idea

Randy (Mr. Romeo) told me about this plan to become serious with his high school sweetheart; he said they had a bond, and when the timing was right, they would become one. He said he wanted to find three poems that reflected his feelings towards her and wanted me to write them on the card. So, she wouldn't know it was me until he gave her the last card of three.

I agreed and thought about doing this, too, and see if she was ready to comment. I finally saw her growing up and graduate nursing school and worked full time at one of the local hospitals. I figured it had been over three years. I've been caring for this woman, and it was time to let her know if she didn't know already. We went to the bookstore and picked out our books and cards to pick the poems.

Does Your Roommate Like Boys

I walked into the Sportsman's and told Jimmy; I'm all his; the old man cut the cord.

Jimmy said, "You have other problems."

I found out one of the bartenders that wanted to screw around with Randy decided once she was turned down to start spreading rumors that we were gay, and her proof was we lived together. I responded to Jimmy, "I think that's funny because that MF'er wakes me up with his conquests; wait till he hears about this; he's going to be pissed."

Randy came into the bar early, and she was working tonight, and I ran over to him and jumped in his arms and kissed him on his forehead, and whispered, your crush thinks we're gay. Randy dropped me and said, don't you ever do that again.

As the night progressed, I would go through darts at Randy like, "don't drink too much. We have to get up early tomorrow, or did you do the dishes before you left. Jimmy was laughing and giving him a hard time also. I found myself surrounded by girls that knew me saying, "We know you're not gay, but the question is out for Randy."

I told Jimmy, "Do you mind I stop this bullshit the only way I could; you could lose a bartender today; I got to go home with him (that didn't sound right)." Jimmy said, "Fuck her

You'll do me a favor because I was going to fire her anyway.

I was doing my promotions, and I commented on a rumor going around questioning my manhood along with my roommate. I have to clear up something personal, and I think it's pretty funny; I asked the bartender it sucks when the town gigolo won't play hot dogs and donuts with you. Now you have to revert to kindergarten rules and call him names; the funny thing is we always thought you liked girls because you still turned down my advancements (drop the needle onto a song).

Jimmy came up to me and gave me a doctor's pepper and said, don't worry, I made it, and by the way, she gave her notice because after your true confessions, the customers started giving her a hard time, and she left.

The Mail Is Out

Well, the mission is complete, we just delivered the last of his mail, and I had my cousin's kids delivered for me since they live two doors down. I told her to come over for dinner next week.

Randy told me he set something up similar to his girl. Now we sit back and wait, what a couple of romantics.

The Verdict Is In

Randy told me today that he struck out, but her girlfriend found it very romantic, and we got her blessing to go out on a date. So, it wasn't the target, but it worked for him.

I called her to confirm tonight, and I didn't get an answer. The last time I called, her sister told me she was working late at the hospital. I took that as my answer, time to move on.

Strippers But The Wrong Sex

Tonight, was Jimmy's big bone he threw to his girlfriend, let them be men.

A male revue and all the male employees were mandatory to work so that the ladies can enjoy a night off. All I know, these women get wild like they never saw a semi-nude dude pushing their junk in their faces.

After the show was over and everything was settling down, Jimmy was buying us Dr. Pepper's, I saw this girl sitting alone, and she looked familiar.

She talked about how her boyfriend was a male dancer, and she was bored with the show because she gets this at night. I said to myself, "Strike THREE, YOUR OUT."

The funny thing was she was a chubby, and I didn't believe a word she was saying; all she had to say was, you're not getting anything tonight.

He's Gone

Randy told me tonight he was moving out because he got let go at the club and couldn't make rent anymore. I was cool with that and understood. Now I would be able to sleep at night without interruption.

Who's Rocking The Boat Now

After the morning show, I got pulled into the boss's office today and said they were going in a different direction. My position would be eliminated, Ruth Ann was leaving, and they hired an executive producer for both parts.

I ask Mr. M what that leaves me; he said, "I'm not firing you. I'm just reassigning you. You will keep doing production and all of the coach's shows as you were before, and you can keep losing weight on me (I was on Nutra System through the station promotion).

He also added, you did a great job in the past year, or I would have cut you out completely; when I find good talent, I make it work, not get rid of them." I left the office feeling good but sort of sad about missing the morning show, not getting up at 4:30 every morning.

Where's My BJ?

It's a quiet Sunday night, and I had low energy; suddenly, Jimmy comes out of the kitchen, "I thought I'm paying for a BJ, not to have the jukebox on." "Hey Ronald McDonald, go back and flip your burgers and leave the adults in the room alone. Have we still pissed your Eagles lost again," I responded? "Now there's my BJ," and he went back to the kitchen.

I Got the Wrong Guy

It was a light Thursday night, and that didn't stop the beer muscle rage. I heard Jimmy and a customer getting loud, and that's like Jimmy before I knew it, those two were at it, and Bobby (the bouncer had this kid on the floor, and all I heard was he was a trooper, and I cupped his arm as he was ready to clock this guy. Bobby got up and got in my face, "He hit Jimmy, and I don't care if he was a trooper." Before we knew it, the local police were storming in, and the sergeant told the trooper, To SHUT THE FUCK UP, and I know your superior, you fucking boot."

We just turned to each other and went, "WOW."

After the dust cleared, Jimmy laughed and said I could finally sue somebody and press charges on them.

After the Dust Cleared

I came in tonight, and Jimmy told me that the trooper had pressed charges against him and the bar for using inappropriate laugh at a wrong time.

I said what. "I told him to get the fuck out of my bar before midnight," Jimmy explained.

I just handed the golden softball, I can't let this one slide, so at 11:59, I asked the bar, do they know, "What time it is," and right at 12, they responded, "IT'S 12 FUCKING CLOCK!!!!" I felt like it was like a scene out of Cheers when Norm walked into the bar. I did see Jimmy laugh, and he came over and asked if I would never do that again because of the legal matter, but he did say, "That's my BJ."

End Of A Run

Sportsman's have been a little light in the crowd the past month, I figured it was new bars opening up, but Jimmy was not acting himself.

At the end of the night, Jimmy pulled me into his office and explained economics to me. He wanted to try something new. He told me this brother and sister DJ team undercut your cost, and I figure I would try them.

I had no problem; I knew it wasn't me, but when the bar takes a turn down, the owner always looks at something to blame. I thanked him for the chance, and we made magic; hopefully, they can do the same.

Reflection Time

What a ride, like they say, only if I knew then what I know now, but I feel being naive help shape me into the man I am now. It would be best if you experienced the school of hard knocks to grow as an individual firsthand.

The business I chose, I knew you did not get settled in, because you're lucky to last a couple of months, me I rode it for close to 6 years, and every stumble I took, I just accepted it and moved on; some would have to hold a boo who party. I felt

I chose a very narcissistic, backstabbing, demanding profession; instead of embracing others that love or enjoy the same journey, they are ready to squash your dreams because they are afraid you will step in and take their spot.

I was lucky when I left either the radio or the bar circuit; I was always welcomed to come back. I wasn't the best, but I knew my spot in the food chain and welcomed the competition and embraced others that wanted a piece of the madness. If talented people surround you, it will bring out the best in one.

I learned out of all the people who rode the wave with me that I could only trust one, and after 30 years, we stayed up late talking on the phone like little girls until 3 in the morning. You knew him as Pork Chops, but I know him as a true friend or just Dave.

As it goes for her, to this day, 30 years later, we still hit and miss. I never sealed the deal, but it seems I can't say goodbye. I look at it as bad timing as it goes to those love poems, I found out later that she didn't know I sent them, but she did have to work late that day. I found out some scumbag at the hospital claimed that he was sending the poems and the big question was, did he reek the rewards.

She did tell me he was a jerk, and she wished she knew it was me, but I still got nothing.

The day I walked out of the Rock was the last time, and I never looked back. I think that run ran its course, and it was time for me and the bar to say goodbye.

The funny thing is I did go back once and was escorted by her. I felt out of place, and the old man, the phony he was, acted like everything was like the first time.

I found myself reconnecting with Jimmy when I had scheduling free from the radio station. I heard Jimmy stop having music, and I went in and talked to him about trying it again.

He replied, "I should have just road it out before because the two ruined my business, all that to save a buck." To me, that's the cut-throat business that is underpriced, usually isn't worth the full price, and you get what you pay for.

You say, oh, there's more, that was the beginning of my tail; I'll have to stop by later and tell you where the road led me today until they keep walking straight. Yes, just a tease, the door was left open at the Sportsman, but that tail would be told later.

I also developed djchronicles.net, an online DJ interactive source for the pro, beginner, or hobbyist as I wrote this journal. In addition, yes, I did become a member of the YouTube generation at DJ Chronicles featuring the best in new rock and dance music.

www.ingramcontent.com/pod-product-compliance
Lightning Source LLC
Chambersburg PA
CBHW051429290426
44109CB00016B/1481